Pilgrim, Aubrey.

Build your own low-
cost PC and save a
bundle.

$29.95

DATE			

Build Your Own Low-Cost PC and Save a Bundle

2nd Edition

This book is dedicated to
all of those hardy trail-blazing computer pioneers
whose endeavors have made our lives so much better.

Build Your Own Low-Cost PC and Save a Bundle

2nd Edition

Aubrey Pilgrim

WINDCREST®/McGRAW-HILL

SECOND EDITION
FIRST PRINTING

© 1993 by **TAB Books**
TAB Books is a division of McGraw-Hill, Inc.
The title of the first edition of this book is *Build Your Own 80286 IBM Compatible and Save a Bundle* (No. 3031).

Library of Congress Cataloging-in-Publication Data

Pilgrim, Aubrey.
   Build your own low-cost PC and save a bundle / by Aubrey Pilgrim.
     p. cm.
   Includes index.
   ISBN 0-8306-4086-X   ISBN 0-8306-4087-8 (pbk.)
    1. Microcomputers—Design and construction—Amateurs' manuals.
   I. Title.
   TK9969.P567 1992
   004.165—dc20   92-26118
                                     CIP

Supervising Editor: Lori Flaherty
Editor: Laura J. Bader
Director of Production: Katherine G. Brown
Designer: Jaclyn J. Boone
Cover design and illustration: Sandra Blair Design, Harrisburg, Pa.   EL1

Contents

2   How to assemble a 286 or 386SX   11

3   Upgrading an older computer   33

4   Motherboards and plug-in boards   45

Introduction

It takes no special training or knowledge to assemble your own computer. I will show how you can easily build your own economical 286 or 386SX computer. Anyone —man, woman, or child—can do it. Computers were once considered a man's domain, especially when it came to assembling one. But more women use them than men. In the factories where computers are assembled, more women are on the assembly line than men. My point is that computer technology does not belong exclusively to men. Many women bought the first edition of this book and built their own computers. Even teenagers have used it to build their own computers for high school and college.

Easy to build

It is very simple to assemble your own computer. You don't need to know anything about electronics. You don't have to do any wiring or soldering, and you don't need any electronic test equipment. With just pliers and a screwdriver, you can build your own computer. Figure I-1 shows some suggested tools. (The bent screwdriver is for prying up chips to replace them. You might never need it.) You can save a bundle of money by doing it yourself.

It takes little time to assemble a system. Once you have purchased the components, it will probably take less than an hour to assemble them. You can gain valuable knowledge about the insides of a computer. You can also gain a valuable sense of pride in doing it yourself. The following chapters have lots of photos and simple in structions to help you build your own computer.

286 or 386SX—Ideal for most purposes

Someone once said, "The person who dies with the most toys wins." By extension this statement can be paraphrased, "The person who dies with the most powerful and fastest computer wins." Many computerphiles yearn for more and more power and faster speed—whether they actually need it or not. Often, they don't need it. It is something like having a 400-horsepower, 12-cylinder engine in a car that is only used once or twice a week to drive to the grocery store.

There are more than 70 million personal computers in use today. A large majority of those sold prior to 1990 were based on the 286 CPU (central processing unit). It is not the most powerful or fastest personal computer (PC), but for most ordinary needs, the 286 is more than sufficient. When you consider its power and versatility, the 286 is the best all-around PC available. It can also be the least expensive. That is, if you build it yourself. However, a 286-type computer can be quite expensive if you buy a 286 PS/1 system from IBM or one of the other brand-name 286 systems. You can assemble a system for about one-third the cost of an equivalent IBM or Apple system.

Except for a few high-end programs, the 286 can run all the programs the 386 or 486 can run. It is not quite as fast and it can't run in the 386 enhanced mode. This is a mode that lets the 386 and 486 use vast amounts of memory. But you can access up to 16 megabytes (Mb) of extended memory with the 286. That is plenty for most ordinary applications. If that is not enough, you can address up to 32Mb using expanded memory.

I-1 Some suggested tools. The plastic bag is great for protecting your software from dirt or dust.

Use this book to build a 386SX

If you must run high-end programs in the 386 enhanced mode, you can use this book to build a low-cost 386SX. The 386SX can run in the 386 enhanced mode and is just a bit faster than a 286 system. Figure I-2 is a 386SX system. On the outside, it looks no different than a 286 or 486. The main difference is the motherboard. You can even use this book to build a 486 system.

Primary difference in PCs

The primary difference in all PCs is the motherboard. Except for the motherboard, a 286 can have the same configuration and components as a 386SX, 386DX, 486SX, or 486DX. The main difference is in the cost of the motherboard. If you build your own computer, that will be the only difference.

Cost to build a system

It is difficult to state an exact cost for a system because prices change almost daily. Another factor is the large number of options available. A system can be configured

I-2 A 386SX computer. From the outside it looks the same as the 286, 386, or 486.

in thousands of different ways by adding different boards, disk drives, monitors, accessories, and peripherals.

The most crucial cost-determining factor is the cost of the CPU. Intel developed the first 286 and 386. They licensed the manufacture of the 286 to several other companies, but they retained the exclusive rights to the 386 and have been the sole source. The fact that Intel had no competition kept the price of the 386 chips very high. But the price is now tumbling down because Advanced Micro Devices (AMD) and Chips and Technology have both been able to clone the 386 CPU. Their versions operate faster and use less power than Intel's versions. This competition is great. It forces the competitors to improve and upgrade their CPUs and to lower prices.

For less than $1100 you can have a 100Mb hard disk, a floppy drive, and a good color monitor. If you can get by with a 40Mb hard disk, a single floppy, and a monochrome monitor, it will cost less than $800. There is more about prices in chapter 2.

One way to determine cost is to look at the ads for components in computer magazines such as *Computer Shopper*, *PC Sources*, and *Computer Buying World*.

Simple assembly

The actual assembly of a 286 or 386SX is very simple. It is merely a matter of connecting the components together. If I covered only the assembly process it would be difficult to fill a book this large. But there is much more to a computer than just a few hardware components. I've provided details about the operations and functions of disk drives, monitors, memory, printers, keyboards, mice, plug-in boards, and other peripherals and accessories. I also discuss some of the essential software that is needed and their applications.

Sources

I mention several companies throughout this book. This does not mean that I endorse those companies to the exclusion of the many other companies that have similar products. I have not had the time nor the opportunity to personally evaluate some of the major hardware items, such as the long list of dot matrix and laser printers. I have relied on the excellent reviews and tests in such magazines as *InfoWorld Direct*, *PC Magazine*, *InfoWorld*, *PC World*, *PC Sources*, *Computer Shopper*, and *Computer Monthly* and in the many other magazines mentioned in chapter 14 for some of my information. In order to keep up with this fast-changing technology, I subscribe to more than 50 computer magazines. If you are serious about keeping up with this ever-changing industry, then you should subscribe to some of the magazines listed in chapter 14.

I attend most national computer shows. The largest is the Computer Dealer Exposition (COMDEX) held in Las Vegas in the fall and in Atlanta or Chicago in the spring. If at all possible, try to attend one of these shows.

If you live near a large city, look for computer swaps. I do most of my buying at swaps. Even if I don't need anything, I sometimes go just for the atmosphere. It is almost like a circus.

Shareware disk —learning to use a computer

It is much easier to assemble a computer than it is to use one. If you are new to computing, you should learn as much as you can about DOS. The latest version of MS-DOS has more than 50 commands, but you will probably never need to know more than 15 or 20. Many colleges and high schools provide regular student classes and adult night classes in DOS and other popular computer programs such as word processors, databases, and spreadsheets.

There are also many companies that hold seminars on how to use various software programs. They might charge $500 to $1000 for a one- or two-day class. I have never gone to one of these seminars because I don't think I could learn enough in one or two days to justify the cost. Besides, if a software program costs $500 or more, you should not have to spend another $500 to learn how to use it.

There is an easier way to learn to use your computer. I have enclosed a coupon for a shareware disk with this book that will make it a lot easier for you to learn. The title of the shareware I recommend is *PCLearn*. The author is Jim Hood, Department PCL 5, P.O. Box 1506, Mercer Island, WA 98040. There are several good books that can help you learn DOS and some of the other basic software programs. TAB Books publishes several good ones. You can reach them at (800)822-8138 for a current catalog.

Don't wait, join the computer generation

If you have been doing without the benefits of a good computer because of the cost, then shame on you. Build your own. You will save a bundle and at the same time you will learn a little bit about this wonderful tool that is changing the lives of all of us.

Thank you for buying my book. I hope you enjoy it.

Chapter 1

Basic components

I am often asked, "What does it cost to build a computer?" and "How much can I save?" That is like asking, "How high is up?"

How much it costs will depend on you—what you want to build, how much you want to spend, and how wisely you shop for the components. The prices are coming down every day. The prices quoted in this book are the prices of today. If you want to wait a month or so, you can get almost any component for less than today's price. But you are also missing out on the advantage of having a computer. So it might be better to spend just a bit more and buy it today.

Helping you make a decision

There are lots and lots of different computers and computer configurations. You can use hundreds and hundreds of different components to configure your computer in almost any way you want. You have to decide what you want to build and what you want to spend. I am going to talk briefly about components to help you make an informed decision, I will go into greater detail about all of the major components in later chapters. I suggest that you read them before making your purchases.

If you have lots of money, then you might not want to build your own computer. If you don't care about saving a bit of money, you can buy an IBM PS/1 or a Macintosh Classic. If you buy one of these machines, you won't have to make many decisions. Most of the decisions are already made for you. You won't have to decide what goodies to add to your system. If you buy a PS/1, the only decisions you'll have to make are whether you want a monochrome or color monitor, and whether you want a hard drive.

If you build your own, you have hundreds of options as to what hardware and accessories to buy. You can configure your computer in a large variety of ways. You have to decide how much memory you want, what size hard disk, the kind of monitor and keyboard, and many other options. The components are standard and all are interchangeable. If you are a little short of money, you can start off with a minimum system and add to it later. You can build a 286 or 386SX computer that has more power, is faster, and has more functionality than the IBM PS/1 or the Macintosh Classic, and you can do it for less than half of what they cost. The main difference is that it will not have the IBM or Apple logo on it.

You don't have
to be an electronics engineer

You might be hesitant as to whether you can build your own computer. However, no electronics experience or any special expertise or skills are required. You need only pliers and a couple of screwdrivers and the ability to follow simple instructions.

The components are all interchangeable. You can shop for the best price on individual components and then assemble them yourself. Once you buy the components, you can put them together in less than an hour. It requires no soldering, wiring, or electronic test equipment. Anybody can do it.

If you are still hesitant, you can buy a bare-bones system, which is usually just a case, power supply, and motherboard. These are the major components, but you still need more components in order to have a functioning computer. You need a keyboard, disk drives, monitor, and monitor adapter. This book shows you how to assemble a computer from scratch or add to a bare-bones system and shows you how to configure it to your needs. This book has hundreds of close-up photos showing what is inside a 286 or 386SX. Along with the photos are step-by-step instructions on how to assemble your own computer.

Building and operating a computer is easy

You don't have to be an automotive engineer to drive a car. Nor do you have to know the detailed operation and physics of an internal combustion engine to be able to drive. Neither is it necessary for you to be a computer scientist to assemble a computer or be a programmer in order to use a computer. Anyone can take advantage of the many thousands of things that a computer can do.

There are thousands of off-the-shelf application programs and software that are very user friendly, especially now that Windows is available. We also have the luxury of being able to address vast amounts of inexpensive RAM (random-access memory). The 286 and 386SX can directly address 16Mb of RAM. What a great leap forward from the 64K limitation that we had to live with in the CP/M world just a few short years ago.

IBM compatibility and ISA

At one time, when clones were mentioned, the first question asked was, "Is it IBM compatible?" In 1990, 24 million personal computers were sold. Of that, IBM sold 2,856,000. The clones, including NEC and Compaq, sold 17,640,000. Because there are several million more clones than IBMs, maybe the question should be reversed.

IBM, with their high prices, continues to lose market shares. Apple's market share has also eroded somewhat. In 1990, Apple sold 1,800,000 units or about 7.5% of the total sold. IBM and Apple have always been bitter rivals, but in October 1991, IBM and Apple formed a joint venture company to share software and technology. They have the money and facilities to carry on research that will help the industry. But it might not help them capture as much of the market as they would like. Most ISA (industry standard architecture) manufacturers are not too concerned. Because of their policies and distribution systems, IBM and Apple will always be overpriced compared to the clones.

IBM created a standard with the PC, XT, and AT. Millions of clone compatibles were built to this standard. The clones began to erode some of IBM's share, so they introduced their PS/2 models on 2 April 1987. In doing so, they abandoned the standard that they created. They also abandoned the billions of dollars worth of hardware that had been developed for the IBM standard. They hoped that everyone would follow them and adopt the new PS/2 microchannel architecture (MCA). But this hardware was single-source, had no competition, and was typically IBM expensive.

Though MCA systems offer a few advantages, most people realize that they can do the same computing with the much less expensive clone-type systems. Most of the IBM PS/2 systems are sold to large corporations and businesses that can write off the costs and those that don't worry too much about budgets.

The old IBM standard is now called the *ISA*. The question of compatibility is no longer an issue. All ISA systems are hardware compatible and interchangeable with each other and with the original IBMs. The PS/1 and PS/2 systems are not hardware compatible with ISA and the original IBM systems. See Fig. 1-1 for a comparison of the standard IBM-type board and the MCA type. Most DOS software is compatible with ISA and all IBM systems.

1-1 Board in upper photo has the standard edge card connector. The board in the lower photo has the small microchannel edge connector.

Macintosh versus ISA

There is no question that the Macintosh, with its icons and mouse, has been the easiest and simplest machine to use. Apple has no competition, so they have always been much more expensive than the clones. Windows, and other new software and technologies, now allows the PC and MS-DOS world to enjoy the same ease of use as the Macintosh.

For every Macintosh in existence, there are about 10 IBM and ISA compatibles. Naturally, most software developers are going to design for the market where they can sell the most. Therefore, much more software has been developed for the larger numbers of ISA-type users.

Even though IBM and Apple have formed a single company, another reason to consider an ISA compatible is that IBM and Apple are only single companies. Hundreds of companies that make ISA compatibles makes for lots of competition, which makes ISA systems much less expensive.

At this time, a good Macintosh costs about $2400. You can assemble a 286 or 386SX for about one-third of what an equivalent Macintosh would cost. You can gain invaluable experience and knowledge if you do it yourself and save a bundle in the process.

Components needed

I will list and briefly discuss all of the major components. Later chapters will go into much more detail about each of them. If you are new to computing, these chapters should help you make better purchase decisions. I will discuss the assembly of a system in the next chapter, but I recommend that you read the chapters on the major components before buying them.

All of the PCs use the same basic components. The main difference is the motherboard and the CPU. Because the components are all interchangeable, you can shop around for the best buys. You can look at the ads in computer magazines such as *Computer Shopper, PC Sources, InfoWorld Direct, Computer Monthly*, and others for an idea of what is available. These ads also give you an idea of the cost of the various components and options. You can order the components through the mail, or if you live near a large city, go to a swap meet or to a local store.

Case and power supply

Several types of cases are available. A few of the different cases are shown in Fig. 1-2. You can use whichever type you prefer. The desktop type is still the most popular. Most desktop types are limited to three or four bays for mounting disk drives. If you want to install two hard disks and a 1.2Mb and 1.44Mb floppy, you need one with at least four bays. Depending on your needs, you might want to buy a tower case. A tower case sits on the floor, and the larger ones might have space for up to eight drive bays. This provides room for two hard drives, two floppies, a tape backup, a CD-ROM, a write-once read-many (WORM) drive, and others.

Many cases are sold with the power supply. Make sure that the power supply is at least 200 watts.

Motherboards

The motherboard is the main board in the computer. It has the all-important CPU, provisions for memory, slots for the plug-in boards, and a built-in clock, and it can have several other built-in functions such as parallel and serial ports, an IDE (integrated disk electronics) interface for hard disks, and other goodies.

1-2   Some different sizes and types of cases.

The original standard-size AT or 286 motherboard was larger than the XT, but most of them are now "baby" size or about the same size as the XT. The hundreds of manufacturers of 286 motherboards offer many options.

The original 386 and 486 motherboards were the larger standard size. But many manufacturers now have the baby sizes. Most 386SX motherboards are the baby size. See chapter 4 for more information about motherboards and plug-in boards.

Memory

When a computer runs a program, the program is loaded into memory and is processed there. When the processing is completed, it is loaded back on the hard disk, printed out, or sent to wherever you want it to go. Many of today's programs require 2Mb or more of memory in order to run. Chapter 5 goes into detail about the many types of memory.

Floppy disk drives

You could get by with a single 360K floppy drive, but I recommend that you buy a 1.2Mb drive. A 1.2Mb drive can read and write to both 360K and 1.2Mb diskettes. You can store 3½ times more data on a 1.2Mb diskette than on a 360K diskette. The 360K drives cost about $50, the 1.2Mb about $55.

I also recommend that you buy a 1.44Mb 3½-inch drive. It can read and write to 720K diskettes as well as 1.44Mb diskettes. The 1.44Mb drives also cost about $55, about $5 more than the 720K drives. Both the 360K and 720K drives are obsolete. I do not recommend that you buy them.

You might have to buy a controller board for you r floppy drives. If you have a hard drive, it might also have a floppy controller built in. If not, you can buy a floppy controller for about $20. You might not need a controller if your motherboard has a built-in IDE interface. See chapter 6 for more details on floppy drives.

Hard disk drives

It is possible to operate a computer without a hard disk, but it is difficult to do much productive work. If your time is worth anything at all, a hard disk can pay for itself in a very short time.

The several hard disk manufacturers have hundreds of different models, sizes, and types of hard disks. An IDE drive has all the controller electronics on the drive itself. However, it still needs an interface to the system. This interface can be built-in on the motherboard, or you can buy a low-cost interface that plugs into one of the slots. Other hard drives need a controller on a plug-in board. In many cases, the controller is made by a company other than the one that manufactures the hard drive. Because the controllers for the IDE drives are made and matched by the same manufacturer, they might operate a bit better. They can also cost a bit less than buying a drive and a separate controller. See chapter 7 for more details on hard drives.

Backup

It is very important that you keep copies or backups of all of your software programs and important data. You never know when your hard disk might crash or have a failure. You can lose some very important data in thousands of ways. You should always have a current backup. You can choose from many methods of backup, some using hardware and some requiring special software programs. See chapter 8 for more details.

Keyboards

The keyboard is a very important part of the computer. It is the main device for communicating with the computer. The many manufacturers have slight differences in the placement of the keys, the tactility, and special adjuncts such as trackballs, calculators, and keypads.

To run Windows and other graphical user interface (GUI) programs, it is essential to have a mouse, trackball, or other pointing device. Chapter 9 discusses keyboards and other input devices in some detail.

Modems, fax, and communications

You can use your computer to communicate with millions of other computers using on-line services and a host of other services. You can download software from bulletin boards or you can send low-cost faxes to millions of other fax sites.

You definitely need some communications hardware and software if you want to get the most from your computer. I will discuss communications in chapter 10.

Monitors

You can use a large variety of monitors. You can buy a monochrome monitor for about $65. I like color even if I am just doing word processing, so I am willing to pay a little more for color. You can buy a good EGA (enhanced graphics adapter) color monitor for about $200. A better VGA (video graphics adapter) monitor will cost about $300. Or you can spend up to $3000 or more for a large screen, very high-resolution monitor.

Monitor adapters

You need a plug-in adapter board to drive the monitor. (Some motherboards have a build-in adapter.) It can cost as little as $20 for a monochrome adapter. You should be able to buy one for standard VGA color for about $75. For very high-resolution color it can cost up to $600. See chapter 11 for more details on monitors and adapters.

Printers

You have lots of options when it comes to buying your printer. You can choose from several manufacturers and hundreds of different types and models, including dot matrix, lasers, inkjets, daisywheels, and many others. Some types are better for a particular application than others, so it depends on what you want to do with your computer and how much you want to spend. Chapter 12 discusses the various types of printers.

Business uses

You can use your computer in thousands of ways. Chapter 13 lists just a few of them.

Software

You need software for your computer. Before you even turn it on, you need operating software such as MS-DOS or DR-DOS. Billions of dollars worth of off-the-shelf software are available. Some of the commercial programs might be a bit expensive. Inexpensive public domain and shareware programs can do just about everything the commercial programs do. See chapter 14 for some software recommendations.

Sources

You might need to know where to buy all of the components that you will need to build your own computer. If you live near a large city, local stores probably sell the parts.

Also most large cities have frequent computer swaps. A computer swap is just a gathering of local vendors at a fairgrounds, a stadium, or some other area. The vendors usually set up booths and tables and present their wares. You can usually find all that you need at these meets. You can go from booth to booth and compare the components and prices. The prices are usually very competitive, and you might even be able to haggle a bit with the vendors.

The other good source for components is through mail order. Just look at the ads in any of the computer magazines. At one time, mail order was a bit risky, but it is fairly safe today. See chapter 15 for more details on magazines, mail order, and other sources.

Troubleshooting

You shouldn't have any problems assembling your computer. If you do, turn to chapter 16 for help and suggestions.

Cost to build different systems

Except for the motherboard, you need about the same basic components in an XT, 286, 386SX, 386DX, 486SX, or 486DX machine. Table 1-1 gives a list of components along with approximate prices. Prices vary widely among the various vendors. The amount of memory, speed of memory, caching, monitor type and size, and many, many other options will affect the price. Table 1-1 shows what it might cost to build any of the computers I have discussed. Note that except for the motherboard, all of the other components are the same.

Table 1-1.

Component	XT	286	386SX	386DX	486SX or DX
Motherboard	$ 45– 100	$ 70– 200	$200– 600	$350– 950	$1000–3500
Case	30– 150	30– 150	30– 150	30– 150	30– 150
Power supply	50– 100	50– 100	50– 100	50– 100	50– 100
Keyboard	30– 150	30– 150	30– 150	30– 150	30– 150
Monitor	65–3000	65–3000	65–3000	65–3000	65–3000
Mon. adapter	50– 600	50– 600	50– 600	50– 600	50– 600
Floppy 1.2Mb	50– 125	50– 125	50– 125	50– 125	50– 125
Floppy 1.4Mb	50– 125	50– 125	50– 125	50– 125	50– 125
Hard drive	150–1500	150–1500	150–1500	150–1500	150–1500
HD, controller	0– 300	0– 300	0– 300	0– 300	0– 300
TOTAL	$520–6150	$545–6250	$675–6650	$825–7000	$1475–9550

Again, the prices in Table 1-1 are only approximate. Prices change daily, usually downward. The computer business is about the only area where prices go down instead of up.

As you can see, you can have a wide variation in the cost depending on the components you choose. For instance, you might not want to install both 1.2Mb and 1.44Mb floppies. You might not need a Super VGA high-resolution 30-inch monitor that might cost $3000, or a 2-gigabyte (Gb) very fast hard disk. Brand names and where you purchase the components also make a big difference. An off-brand component from a small company might perform as well as one with a big-company brand name. Some larger companies charge twice as much for the same component

as smaller companies. As long as the device is designed properly, those little electrons inside the circuit don't care diddly about the brand name. The hard drive controller (HD controller) might cost nothing if it is built-in on the motherboard.

You might see bare-bones systems advertised for less than the minimum shown
in Table 1-1, but you should read the ads carefully. The system might be without a
monitor, memory, or even a CPU. You have to shop wisely. Incidentally, many of the
ads I have seen for low-priced Macintosh systems usually have some small print that
says, "without keyboard and monitor."

You can add about $7 billion worth of peripherals, components, and boards to
your computer. These items allow you to configure your computer in hundreds of different ways. You might want to add several of them later, but the basic items can get
you up and computing.

Chapter 2

How to assemble a 286 or 386SX

I mentioned earlier that all PCs are essentially the same except for the motherboards. The instructions and photos in this chapter can be used as a guide to assemble a 286, a 386SX, or even a 486, depending on which motherboard you buy.

I mention AT-type systems throughout this book. An AT-type system can be a 286, 386, or 486. I also mention ISA (industry standard architecture). ISA used to be known as the IBM compatible system.

No matter which system you choose to build, they are all assembled in basically the same way. The assembly does not require any special expertise or electronics knowledge. It requires no soldering and you need only pliers and a screwdriver and about an hour to do the job. The assembly primarily consists of plugging in cables and boards. For this hour of assembly time you can save from $500 to $1500. How much you save will depend on how well you shop and the components you buy. Some brand-name products can cost twice as much or more than a no-name product. In most cases, the no-name product will perform as well as the high-priced brand-name product.

Preassembly

There are several different versions and manufacturers of motherboards, disk drives, and other components. The components you buy might not look like those shown in the photos in this chapter. Some might have more installed goodies than others, but basically they all work the same.

You should make sure to get as much information as possible about any component you buy. You should have a small booklet or some sort of documentation showing the location of the various connectors, switches, and jumpers that must be set up to configure your system. For instance, you might have two or more serial and parallel ports built into your motherboard. Pins are mounted on the motherboard that accept connectors and cables for the ports. There are usually other pins that have small shorting bars to enable or disable these ports. Some systems have a switch or pins with a shorting bar for changing the system speed. There might also be pins to configure the board for the type of monitor you are using—monochrome, color, EGA, or VGA. Without the instruction booklet and diagrams, it might be very difficult to configure your system. Some of the newer motherboards allow many of these configurations to be done externally from the keyboard.

Benchtop test

Before I go to the trouble of installing a system, I lay everything out on a bench and connect it together. I then apply power to make sure that everything is working. If it doesn't work, it is much easier to troubleshoot when it is out in the open.

Once the motherboard has been configured to your requirements, you can install the plug-in boards, keyboard, disk drives, and monitor. You can then turn the power on and see if everything works.

Figure 2-1 shows all of the components needed for a basic system. Figure 2-2 is a photo of a standard-size AT motherboard. Your motherboard might not look like this one. There are hundreds of different manufacturers, but basically motherboards are all much the same. You might buy a motherboard with built-in functions such as an IDE controller for floppy and hard disks. In this case, there is probably a set of pins on the board for the cables from the disk drives.

2-1 Components needed for a 286 or 386SX.

2-2 A standard-size 286 motherboard.

Figure 2-3 shows the power supply being connected to the motherboard. These power supply connectors are usually marked P8 and P9. Figure 2-4 is a close-up of these two connectors. Note that the two black wires on each connector must be adjacent to each other in the center of the connection. It is very important that these connectors be connected properly, otherwise the components on the motherboard could be severely damaged when power is applied.

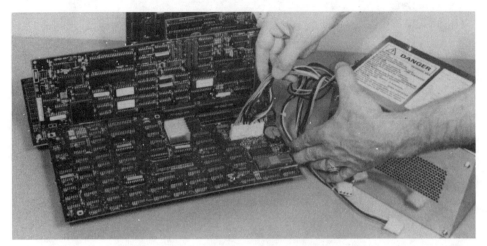

2-3   Connecting a power supply to a motherboard.

2-4   A close-up of a motherboard's power connectors.

Figure 2-5 shows a 34-wire controller cable being attached to a hard disk edge connector. (It is called an edge connector because it is formed from an edge of the circuit board.) The cable has a red, blue, or some other colored wire on one side to indicate pin 1. In some cases the cable has a key in it and there is a slot in the edge connector so that it can only be plugged in properly. The edge connector has a slot between pins 2 and 3 for the key. Without a key, the cable could be plugged in backwards. The edge connector on the hard disk usually has a 1 or a 2 etched on the board. (All the even numbers of the edge connector are on one side of the board and all of the odd numbers are on the other side.) Plug the cable in so that the colored wire goes to the end of the edge connector marked 1 or 2. If there is no marking, just look for the slot on the edge connector and plug the cable in so that the colored wire is on that side.

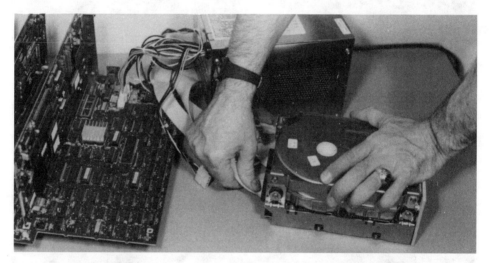

2-5   A 34-pin ribbon cable connector being attached to a hard disk.

There is also a 20-wire data cable that plugs into an edge connector on the back of the hard disk. This cable also has a colored wire that indicates pin 1. Use the same procedure as just mentioned. Look for an etched 1 or 2 on the edge connector and plug it in so that the colored wire goes to that side of the connection. This edge connector also has a key slot between pins 2 and 3. The IDE hard disks have a single 40-wire cable. Most of them are keyed so that they can only be plugged in properly.

Figure 2-6 shows the attachment of the power cable from the power supply. There are four identical cables from the power supply so it is possible to power two hard disks and two floppy disks or any combination. The connectors on these cables are shaped so that they can only be plugged in the proper way.

Figure 2-7 shows the other ends of the two cables for the hard disk before they are attached to the controller board. This controller board can control two floppy drives and two hard disk drives. The controller card has two 34-pin connectors and two 20-pin connectors. The 34-pin connector toward the back of the board is for the cable to the floppy disk drives. When plugged in properly, the colored wire is on top.

2-6   Attaching a power cable to a hard disk.

2-7   Preparing to attach hard disk cables to a controller card.

There are two connectors on this cable for two floppy drives. This cable is shown in Fig. 2-8. Note that the connector on the end is split and twisted. This connector goes to floppy disk drive A. If a second floppy drive is used, the connector in the middle

2-8 The twisted cable in the front will be plugged into floppy drive A.

plugs into it. These cables also have a colored wire that indicates pin 1, and the edge connector on the floppy drive will be marked with a 1 or a 2.

Referring back to Fig. 2-7, the 34-wire cable for the hard disks might also have two connectors. Both connectors on this cable might be wired identically. If you have two hard disks, the first hard disk (or C drive) should be connected to the end connector. The second hard disk should be connected to the one in the center. The hard disks should have pins (or some other method) that must be shorted to denote drive 1 and drive 2. You should receive some documentation with your hard disk that shows where the pins are. You might receive a 34-wire cable with a twist at the end connector. It looks like the standard cable for a floppy drive, except that different wires are twisted. These hard drive cables are not interchangeable with the floppy cables. With this type of cable, the pins on both hard drives will be shorted as drive 1.

You should have some documentation for the connections to the controller board. Usually, there are markings on the controller. If the controller also has the floppy controller, it will have two identical 34-pin connectors. Make sure that you select the proper one. On most controllers, the 34-pin connection nearest the front of the board is for the hard disk. There should be a marking somewhere indicating pin 1. The colored wire on the cable goes to pin 1.

There are two 20-pin connectors on the controller board for the data cables of the hard disks. There should be some sort of marking on the board indicating hard disk 1 or 2. Usually the 20-pin connector nearest the 34-pin connector is for drive 1. Again, the colored wire should go to pin 1. Figure 2-9 shows the hard disk cables connected to the controller board. Figure 2-10 shows a power cable for the floppy disk drive.

2-9   Hard disk cables connected to the controller card.

2-10   A power cable for a floppy disk drive.

2-11 The 34-pin connector for the floppy disk drive A. There are usually two connectors on this cable. The one on the end with the twisted wires determines drive A.

2-12 Connecting a 34-wire cable connector to drive A. Make sure the colored wire goes to the edge connector end with the slot between pins 2 and 3.

2-13 A system connected on a bench for pretesting before installing in the case.

Figure 2-11 shows the 34-pin connector for the floppy disk drive. Because you have only one floppy, this is drive A. Figure 2-12 shows the connector attached to the floppy drive. Figure 2-13 shows a monitor attached to the monitor driver card. The card in the center is a parallel port for a printer.

The keyboard connector is on the rear of the motherboard, usually near the motherboard power connector. It is small and square and can be seen in Fig. 2-6 between the power cable connection and the plug-in board. Note that the XT- and AT-type keyboards might look identical, but they are different internally. Many of the keyboards have a small switch on the back that can be set for either XT or AT. Many of the newer keyboards can sense the type of computer and switch automatically.

Applying power

You should again check to make sure that all of the cables and plug-in boards are installed correctly. You are now ready to try out your new computer. You will need a boot disk with a copy of MS-DOS or DR-DOS to boot up the machine from drive A. Once DOS is up and running, you can format your hard disk and install the disk operating system on it. See chapter 7 for more information about hard drives. You are now ready to apply power to see if everything operates properly.

Burn in and infant mortality

A few years ago, there were lots of problems with boards and components. Many companies did not spend much time or money on quality control. Also, many new circuits were still untried. But today, the technology has advanced and matured, and there are not nearly as many failures today as in the early days.

If a semiconductor circuit is properly designed, it will last several lifetimes because there are no mechanical parts to wear out. If a semiconductor is defective or the circuit is not properly designed, it might draw too much current, or too much voltage, or be stressed to the extent it fails. A semiconductor will usually fail in the first week or so of operation. This is called *infant mortality*. Most vendors do a "burn in" on their products to help to eliminate infant mortality. This usually entails applying power and operating the product continuously for about 48 hours.

You might want to add a couple more days of continuous power before installing it in the case. If anything fails, it is much easier to find it and get it replaced if it is not in the case. It will help if you use your computer while it is being burned in.

TEST.BAT

You can make a small batch file such as the following to help exercise your computer during the time that you are not using it.

At the C> type the following (at the end of each line, press Enter or Return):

```
COPY CON TEST.BAT
DIR
TEST2
```

then press the F6 key to tell DOS that you have finished this. .BAT file. You should see a message saying that one file has been copied. Now type the following:

```
COPY CON TEST.2BAT
TEST
```

then press F6 to end the file. You should see the same message that a file has been copied.

When you type TEST, it causes the directory to be displayed. Then it causes TEST2.BAT to run, which will run TEST again. This sets up a continuous loop that will run indefinitely. You can stop it at any time by pressing the Ctrl key and the C key. This test is rather simple, but it helps.

Installing in the chassis

Once you are satisfied that the system works, you can install it in the chassis. You will have to disconnect some of the cables and boards in order to do this.

Figure 2-14 shows a case with a plastic bag of small parts, the speaker, rails for the disk drives, plastic standoffs for the motherboard, and other small pieces of hardware. One of the white plastic standoffs can be seen near the speaker. Near the standoff is a slotted cutout for the standoff. Four of these cutouts are on the floor of the case. There are three black plastic standoffs mounted on the floor of the case. They have a slot that accepts the right edge of the motherboard. Because there are so many different systems, yours might not look like this one.

Figure 2-15 shows the back of the motherboard. Four of the white plastic standoffs are pressed into holes from the back. The standoffs have a slotted collar. The

2-14 A 286 chassis and its small parts.

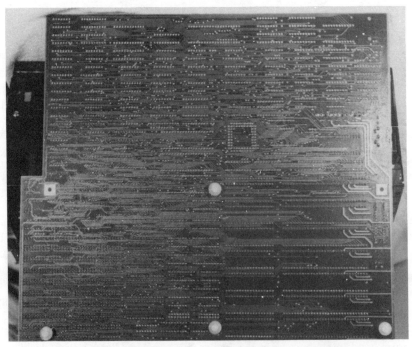

2-15 The back of a motherboard. The white objects are the plastic standoffs.

motherboard is placed on the floor of the case. The standoffs are positioned over the cutouts, are dropped in, and are pushed to the right about one-quarter inch. The small portion of the cutouts lock the white plastic standoffs in place and the right edge of the motherboard is engaged in the horizontal slots of the black standoffs. Screws are then placed in the holes in the front and back center of the motherboard. These two screws hold the motherboard in place and also form a good ground to the case.

Figure 2-16 shows the bottom of the power supply and the bottom of the case. Notice that the power supply has two depressed slots and the case has two raised tongues. The power supply is placed over the raised tongues and slides toward the back of the case. Four screws from the back of the case fasten the power supply securely. Figure 2-17 shows the motherboard mounted in the case and the power supply connected.

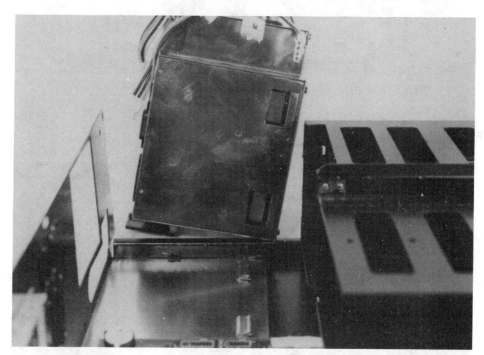

2-16 The bottom of the power supply. Note the slots and the raised tongues on the floor of the chassis to receive these slots.

Figure 2-18 shows a close-up of the power supply connector showing the four black wires in the center. To the left of the power supply connector is the plug-in connector for the keyboard.

Figure 2-19 shows the disk controller card with all the cables attached. The speaker is mounted on a bracket with a single screw. The leads to the speaker and the LED power indicator are plugged into the pins on the front of the motherboard. The leads from the LED for the hard disk indicator are plugged into the pins on the

2-17 The motherboard installed and the power supply cables connected.

2-18 A close-up of a power supply connection. Note that the four black wires are in the center.

2-19 A disk controller card with all cables connected.

front of the disk controller card. You might have several other wire leads from the LEDs and switches on the front panel of the chassis. Your motherboard documentation should show where all of the leads plug in.

Figure 2-20 shows the disk drives and the plastic rails that are attached to them. These rails fit in grooves in the case so that the drives can easily slide in and out.

Figure 2-21 shows the small angle brackets that hold the disk drives in place. The angle presses against the rail of the disk drive so that it is secure. The brackets are inaccessible when the cover of the case is installed so the disk drives cannot be removed without removing the cover. The cover has five screws in the back to hold it on. Most of the newer cases do not use these brackets. They use screws and other methods to keep the disk drives in place.

The key lock performs another useful function. With the power on, the key can be switched to the keyboard lock position and nothing can be entered from the keyboard. If you are in the middle of a job, you can lock out the keyboard, take a break, and not worry about someone fooling around with the computer while you are gone.

Figure 2-22 shows a battery pack attached to the end of the power supply. (Double-sided foam tape was used to attach the battery pack.) The BIOS (basic input/output system) of the AT uses low-current CMOS ROM (complementary metal-oxide semiconductor read-only memory) to hold the system configuration and some of the boot routines. The battery pack used in the IBM PC-AT costs $30 and is only good for about two years. The compatibles and clones use a battery pack with four AA (penlight) alkaline batteries that cost about $1 each. These batteries last about three

2-20 Plastic rails for disk drives. Your system case might not need these rails.

2-21 Small angle brackets used to hold disk drives in place.

years. If you have an older system and you find that you have to reset the date every so often, your battery might need to be replaced. Newer motherboards have a built-in rechargeable battery that should last 5 to 10 years.

Mounting disk drives

The original IBM PC had space for two, full-height floppy drives. With the release of the XT, you could have one full-height floppy and one full-height 10Mb hard disk. But

2-22 A battery pack attached to the case of a power supply. Double-sided foam tape was used to attach it. Your system will probably have a rechargeable battery.

the clones soon came out with half-height drives. It then became possible to mount two floppies and two hard disks in this place. But it was rather difficult and time-consuming to mount the disk drives on the brackets.

It is considerably easier to mount the disk drives on the standard AT case and newer cases. There are grooves in the case for plastic rails that attach to the disk drives. The drives slide in from the front and a small bracket holds them in place.

The standard AT case size is about 1-inch higher than the PC, so it is possible to mount three half-height drives in the open area. There are three grooves in this area. Two grooves in the left hand area make it possible to mount two half-height hard drives or one full-height hard drive. This area on the left is inaccessible when the cover is installed, but ordinarily it is not necessary to access the hard drives. The cover extends over the small brackets that hold the drives in place. This provides some security because the drives cannot be removed without the key to unlock the cover.

Figure 2-23 shows a 3½-inch disk sitting in the slot beneath a 5¼-inch floppy. Figure 2-24 shows the extenders and rails that must be used to make it fit in the 5¼-inch slot.

Buttoning up the system

Because there are several different versions of motherboards, yours might not look like the ones shown here. You should make sure to get as much information as possible about any components you buy. You should get a small booklet showing the location of the various connectors, switches, and jumpers needed to configure your system. For instance, you might have two or more serial or parallel ports built into

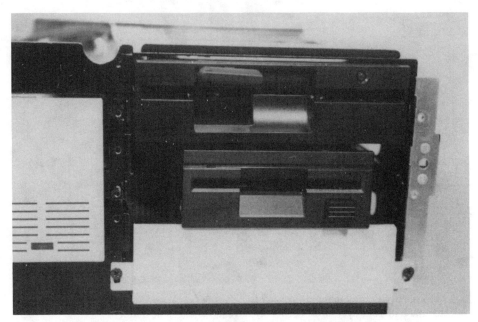

2-23 A 3½-inch floppy drive sitting under a 5¼-inch drive.

2-24 The adapter extenders and rails needed to make a 3½-inch drive fit a 5¼-inch slot. Your system might not need the adapter.

your motherboard. Pins mounted on the motherboard accept connectors and cables for the ports. There are usually other pins that have small shorting bars or switches to enable or disable these ports. There might also be pins or switches for configuring the board to the type of monitor you are using—monochrome, color, EGA, or VGA. Without the instruction booklet and diagrams, it might be very difficult to configure your system. Some of the newer motherboards allow many of these configurations to be done externally from the keyboard.

Once the motherboard is configured to your requirements, you can install the plug-in boards and the cover. But before installing the cover, it is a good idea to double-check all the cable connections and switch settings. You can then plug in the monitor and keyboard. Note that the XT and AT keyboards might look identical, but they are different internally. Many keyboards have a switch on the back that can be set for either XT or AT.

A word of caution

I strongly suggest that you buy a power strip with five or six outlets for all of the peripherals that will be connected to your computer. This is especially important if you are going to use your computer at home. Most newer homes have three-wire outlets so that the plugs are polarized and can only be plugged in one way. Almost all printers, monitors, computers, and other peripherals have the three-wire male power connector. If you are using your computer at home and have only two-wire outlets, you might be tempted to cut off the grounding part of the connector so that you can plug the connector into a two-wire outlet. YOU SHOULD NOT DO THIS. It is possible that some of your units might not be isolated from ground; you could have 110 volts on the case of your printer or some other peripheral. Even if they are isolated, plugging in one or more of your components to the wrong side of the line can cause grounding problems.

The plug-in slots in a two-wire outlet are also polarized. If you look closely at them, you will see that one slot is wider than the other. This slot should be grounded. It will usually have a white wire attached to it. If you follow it back to your fuse box, you might find that it is grounded to a water pipe or some other common ground that eventually goes to earth ground. The other wire, attached to the narrow slot, will be black or some other color. This wire should carry the 110 volts.

Some older houses, and even some new ones, could possibly have some of their connectors miswired. I live in a fairly new apartment and I found several outlets that were miswired. It is an easy matter to check the outlet. Most hardware stores have small, inexpensive voltage indicators. These are usually just a small neon bulb. When it is plugged into a socket it lights up if there is voltage present. Or, you can go to an electronics store and buy a small, inexpensive volt-ohmmeter, a very handy tool to have around the house for any type of appliance electrical problem.

If you have a two-wire system in your house, check the outlet to make sure that it is wired properly. Remove the cover and make sure that the white wire goes to the wider slot. Then buy a power strip and an adapter so that it can be plugged into the two-wire outlet. I suggest that you buy a strip that has surge protection. If you have a refrigerator or other heavy appliances on the line, a large backsurge of voltage can occur in the line when they turn on. These surges can cause glitches that can cause errors in your data.

If you live in an area where lightning storms occur, I suggest that you buy protectors for your system. Check with your local hardware or electrical store. It is a good idea to disconnect the power strip during heavy electrical storms. If you must use your computer when there is a chance of a power outage, you should save your data to disk frequently. Otherwise, if the power goes off even for a split second, all of your data that has not been saved to disk will be lost from RAM. It is a good idea to save your data every 10 to 15 minutes because a glitch, or almost any of a thousand things, can cause you to lose all of the data that has not been saved to disk. After you install your power strip, you are ready to turn on the system and start computing.

Most used and useful DOS commands

If you are new to computing, you should take a course in DOS. Here are just a few important things that you should know.

Data is managed in a computer by categorizing it and placing it in files. A hard disk can be likened to a filing cabinet. The files are similar to those that you might find in a filing cabinet and the disk might be partitioned similar to the different drawers in a file cabinet.

One of the first things to learn is acceptable file names. A file name can have up to eight characters. You can place a period at the end of these eight characters and add up to three more characters as an extension. For instance, you can have a file called DOSNAMES.TUT. The eight characters and the extension can be alphabet characters, numerals, or a mixture. I often use the date as an extension on my letter files. For instance, JOHNDOE.625 tells me that I wrote to John Doe on 25 June. For October, November, and December, I use an O, N, or D with the date, such as JOHNDOE.N25.

There are certain symbols and characters that DOS reserves for itself. The following symbols cannot be used as part of a file name: :, (), [], {}, /, \, <, >, $, !, #, %, ^, *, +, =, –, ", `, ?, @, &, and l. Any word that is a DOS command cannot be used as a file name such as copy, del, erase, restore, backup, assign, xcopy, etc.

There about 50 DOS commands. When I first got into computing. I took a class on DOS. The instructor threw the book at us. He placed the same emphasis on every command and insisted that we learn them all. There are instances when a person might need all 50 commands. I have never had an occasion to use more than 15 or 20 of them over the last 10 years. Some of the most used commands are copy, del, cd, md, rd, prompt, dir, chkdsk, diskcopy, diskcomp, format, and fdisk. These commands can be entered in uppercase (CAPITALS) or lowercase.

It would be very difficult to do any productive computing on a PC without the copy command. You use it to copy files from one disk to another, from one directory to another, to make backups, and to make .bat files.

If you happen to be on drive C and you want to copy a file from drive B to drive A, type copy b:myfile a:myfile. If you are on drive B, you can leave the b: off and type copy myfile a:myfile. Note the space between the name of the file to be copied, myfile, and the target disk, a:.

Note that copy can be a destructive command. For instance, if you already have a file on the a: drive with the name myfile, when you copy the file from b:, it copies over the original myfile and replaces it. The data is gone forever. You can prevent this by typing copy myfile a:myfile1 (or give it any name that you want).

PC learning—a help disk

I don't have the space in this book to go through and explain all of the commands. I have included a disk of a shareware program with this book that should be very helpful to the beginner as well as the experienced user. This disk goes into some detail about the most useful commands. It is also a good tutor for learning about computers. To use the disk, insert it into your drive and type GO. Then use your arrow keys to move across the menu bar at the top to the subject that interests you.

Chapter 3

Upgrading an older computer

The standard PC or XT case is 19.6 inches wide, 16 inches deep, and 5.5 inches high. The standard 286 AT case is 21 inches wide, 16 inches deep, and 6.25 inches high. The AT case is wider than the XT case because the 286 motherboard requires a lot more components and circuitry.

VLSI revolution

Shortly after IBM released their 286 AT, Chips and Technology began designing very large scale integration (VLSI) chips that integrate several of the 286 mother- board functions. They were able to design a single chip that replaces as many as 30 chips on an IBM-type motherboard. By using these chips the size of the 286 mother- board is reduced to the size of the XT. The clone makers immediately came out with a baby 286 motherboard. You can remove the motherboard from a standard IBM PC or XT or one of the compatibles, install the baby 286 motherboard, and have an im- mediate upgrade to a much more powerful machine. Or you can buy the mother- board and standard components and build a small-size 286 in a standard-size case. Because of the developement costs, the board was a bit more expensive than the standard-size 286 board, but they soon became quite reasonable.

About a year after the clones came out with the baby 286 AT, IBM released their own motherboard and system to replace the aging PC-XT. They called it the PC-XT 286.

Converting a PC or XT into an AT

Figures 3-1 and 3-2 show a couple of baby 286 boards. They are slightly different. The one in Fig. 3-2 has a notch in the front because some of the XTs have a disk-mount- ing bracket to the floor of the case. Most XTs have an elevated disk-holding bracket so that the full-sized motherboard shown in Fig. 3-1 can be used. Another difference is that the board in Fig. 3-1 has seven slots with only three 36-pin, 16-bit data con- nectors. The motherboard in Fig. 3-2 has the standard eight slots with 36-pin, 16-bit data connectors.

Figure 3-3 shows the back of the motherboard shown in Fig. 3-1. Seven white plastic standoffs, similar to the ones in the standard AT, have been installed. Two screws, one in front, and one in back, secure the motherboard and make a good ground to the case. The newer XT cases are designed to accept these standoffs. For the older-style cases, nine plastic or brass standoffs must be used.

There are "baby" motherboards for the 286, 386SX, 386DX, 486SX, and 486DX. Using any one of these boards, an XT can be converted into a more powerful machine in about 20 minutes. The greatest difficulty in the entire operation is removing and replacing the five screws in the back that hold the cover on.

Figure 3-4 shows an IBM XT with the cover off, the plug-in boards removed, and the power supply disconnected. Two screws are removed and the XT motherboard is pulled out. Figure 3-5 shows the case with the XT motherboard removed. Note that it is not necessary to remove the power supply, disk drives, or any of the other components.

Figure 3-6 shows the new baby 286 motherboard in place. Figure 3-7 shows the disk drive cables being reconnected to the disk controller boards. Figure 3-8 shows the cables going to the two separate controller boards. The same disk controller

3-1 A motherboard for a baby 286. Note that this board has only seven slots.

3-2 Another motherboard for a baby 286. Note that it has eight slots and that it has a cutout in the front for those XTs cases with a bracket for the disk drives.

3-3 The back of the motherboard shown in Fig. 3-1. Note the white plastic standoffs.

3-4 An IBM XT with the cover and boards removed and the power supply disconnected from the motherboard.

3-5 The case with motherboard removed. This is a later model IBM XT with the raised brackets for the standoffs. The earlier cases did not have this feature.

boards that were used in the XT can be used in the 286. One of the controller boards is for the hard disk, the other is for the floppy drives. This is a disadvantage because it uses two of your precious slots. Another disadvantage is that the older floppy controller can handle only 360K drives. It will not handle 1.2Mb and 1.44Mb drives. Most of the later disk controllers can control both types of floppies and hard disks on a single board. Just a few years ago, these controllers cost more than $200. They are now available for as little as $60. Or you can buy a floppy controller such as the one shown in Fig. 3-9 for as little as $20.

Figure 3-10 shows the IBM with the cover reinstalled. In its previous form, as an IBM PC-XT, the computer operated at 4.77 megahertz (MHz), and was limited to 640K of RAM with all the other limitations of the older technology. Because it was a genuine IBM, it was worth about $600. By using about 20 minutes of time and installing a $100 motherboard, the machine is now worth about $1200.

This machine can now use any of the 16-bit boards and can run Windows and other 16-bit software. As an XT, it idled along at 4.77 MHz. Depending on the speed of the CPU and the motherboard chosen, this machine can operate at speeds of up to 25 MHz.

If you are converting one of the early model IBM PCs, you should check your power supply. The early PCs came with a 67-watt power supply. This is not nearly enough capacity to power two disk drives, hard drives, and eight plug-in boards. A 150- or 200-watt power supply is about the same size as the 67-watt power supply and only costs about $50.

3-6 The new baby 286 motherboard installed.

3-7 Disk drive cables being reconnected.

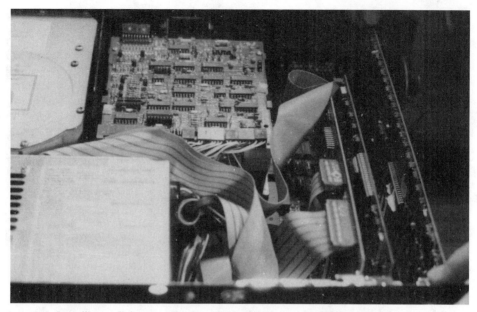

3-8 Installing a disk controller board. Note that the same plug-in cards were used.

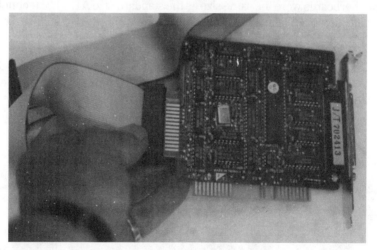

3-9 A small floppy disk controller that can be used in XT- or AT-type computers.

New standard size

Because of the advantages of VLSI, there are very few, if any, manufacturers still making the standard-size 286 motherboard. Almost all 286 motherboards are now the "baby" size. Figure 3-11 shows a baby 286, with no memory, priced at $70. Figure 3-12 shows a 286 motherboard on the left that is even smaller than the standard XT board on the right.

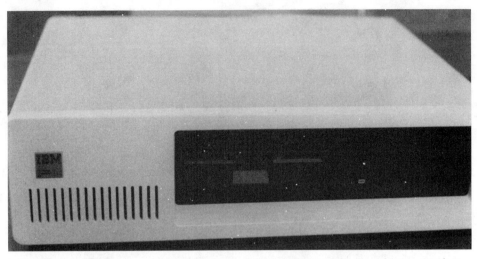

3-10 A new baby 286. Now worth about twice what it was before installing the new motherboard.

Because of the need for added circuitry and electronic components, the early 386
and 486 motherboards were the same size as the standard-size AT. VLSI technology has
advanced considerably. Today, almost all motherboards are the new standard baby size.

Increasing the speed

The IBM PC introduced in 1981 operated at 4.77 MHz, about the same speed as the
CP/M machines. The 8088 CPU processes two 8-bit chunks of data at a time, so they
handle data at almost twice the speed of the CP/M machines. But even at this speed,

3-11 A baby 286 motherboard with no memory.

3-12 A baby 286 motherboard (left) that is much smaller than the XT (right).

they are painfully slow when it comes to handling large spreadsheet files and some graphics programs. Several manufacturers developed plug-in accelerator boards. At about the same time, the clone makers started producing compatible XTs with the Turbo option. With these options, a PC or an XT can operate at as high as 10 MHz or 12 MHz. If you have an older PC or XT and don't want to go all the way up to the 286, you can add one of these boards. You can increase the speed of your PC or XT for as little as $10, all the way up to $1500. But none of these options will give you all of the power, versatility, and flexibility of a real 286 or 386.

NEC V20

The least expensive way to increase the speed of a PC or XT is to remove the 8088 CPU and replace it with an NEC V20. When they were first introduced they sold for as much as $40. They are now down as low as $10 at some discount houses.

The NEC V20 CPU is a direct replacement for the 8088. (In fact, it is so similar that Intel sued NEC.) The V20 handles some types of data a bit faster than the 8088. Some of the early vendors of this chip claimed increases of up to 40 percent, no matter whether you were operating at 4.77 MHz or even 8 MHz. But I have never heard of anyone who achieved this. I bought one and did several benchmark tests. The best I could do was about 10 percent. The type of program that is used makes quite a bit of difference. Some programs will show little or no increase in performance. Some number-crunching programs give the best results. NEC also manufactures a V30 chip that speeds up the 8086 CPU. The IBM PS/2 Model 30 uses the 8086.

The V20 and V30 are available from JDR Microdevices and from several other computer parts and supply stores. Look in any of the computer magazines for ads.

Speeding up an older AT

When IBM introduced the new PC-AT, it was set to operate at 6 MHz. But many people discovered that they could replace the 12-MHz crystal with a 16-MHz crystal and increase the speed to 8 MHz. Unlike the PC and the XT, the AT comes with two separate crystals. It is a very simple matter to change the one that controls the clock speed. Almost all of the clone ATs come with three crystals and a switch so that the frequency can be changed from 6 MHz (from a 12-MHz crystal) to 8 MHz (from a 16-MHz crystal.) This option was provided because some of the older software programs, mostly games, will not run properly at 8 MHz. Almost all software now operates at any frequency.

If you decide to speed up your system by installing higher-speed crystals, make sure that your CPU is capable of operating at the higher frequency. The crystals might cost no more than $2 or $3 each. You can buy several and try the higher frequency, if it doesn't work, install a lower frequency. Some 286 CPUs can now operate at as high as 25 MHz. Crystals are available from JDR Microdevices and from several other computer supply houses.

New BIOS

If you have an older 286, you might have trouble installing a 1.44Mb 3½ inch floppy drive. The BIOS might have been manufactured before the 1.44 Mb was developed. In the early days, Phoenix and Award were the primary developers for clone BIO-chips. They were fairly compatible. You could pull either one off a motherboard and replace it with the other. But now several other companies have developed BIOS chips. The motherboard manufacturers have also added several goodies to their boards to differentiate them from other manufacturers. Many of them now use a custom BIOS that is designed for their boards. Many of the BIOS chips are no longer compatible.

There are several companies that offer BIOS upgrade chip sets. Figure 3-13 shows some BIOS chips. You should be aware that many of them are rather expensive. Some are advertised from $79.95 to $89.95. You can buy a complete 286 motherboard for about $70. You might be able to get a BIOS set from a local dealer for a more reasonable price. If you need to install a new chip, you might need to have an understanding with the vendor that you can return it if it doesn't work.

It is very easy to pull out the old BIOS and plug in a new one. Before you do anything though, make a drawing of the location and orientation of the chips. One end of the chip will have a dot or small indentation to indicate pin 1. The two chips are different, one will be marked "Low" or "Odd" and the other "High or "Even."

Installing a coprocessor

Depending on the type of program you are running, a coprocessor can speed up the processing 100 to 500 percent. If you are running large spreadsheets, databases, or CAD programs, you might need a coprocessor. The software that you use must be designed to utilize the coprocessor, otherwise it does you no good.

Unless you paid extra for your motherboard, it will have an empty socket for the coprocessor. Depending on the speed of your computer, the coprocessor can cost more than the motherboard. The 286 uses the 80287, the 386SX uses the 80387.

3-13 Some BIOS chips.

It is very easy to install a coprocessor. Just look for the empty socket, usually near the CPU, and plug in the coprocessor chip.

Accelerator boards

There are several companies that make plug-in boards that can essentially turn a PC or XT into a 286 or 386 machine. Adding an accelerator board is usually very simple, just plug in the board and replace the CPU. You will then be able to process large spreadsheets, CAD programs, and other CPU-intensive programs.

A drawback to the accelerator board approach is that the XT motherboard has only an 8-bit bus. You will not be able to use any of the plug-in boards designed for the 16-bit 286 or 386. Another consideration is that accelerator boards usually cost as much or more than a 386SX or 386DX motherboard.

There are also accelerator boards that can turn a 286 into a 386DX. It takes only a few minutes longer to install a 386SX or 386DX motherboard. This gives you much more utility and functionality. I do not recommend accelerator boards.

Converting a 286 to a 386SX

Because 286 and 386SXs are both externally 16-bit systems, some companies have developed a small module that can be installed in the 286 CPU socket. The AOX company has developed the StaX SX module (see Fig. 3-14). The module has a 386SX CPU, a BIOS, and some other associated circuitry. It comes in a 16-MHz and a 20-MHz version. It is very easy to install. Just remove the 286 CPU and plug in the module. The AOX company also makes a module that can convert an IBM PS/2 286 into a 386SX. This is well worth the cost.

3-14 A plug-in module from AOX that can convert a 286 into a 386SX.

Installing a processor upgrade

Several companies have developed processor modules that can transform a 286 into a 386SX, which allows you to use all the newest software, such as OS/2, Windows NT, and other 32-bit software.

The Evergreen Technologies Companies (1-800-733-0934) has processor modules and replacement chips that can transform a 286 into a 386 or 486. The chips can be installed in most ISA clone-type machines and in the 286-based PS/2s. They use an Intel chip for the 386 and a Cyrix chip for the 486 conversion. See Figs. 3-3 and 3-4. This is a very easy upgrade. Just pull the cover, locate the 286 CPU, and plug in the new module.

The following are a few of the other companies who make processor modules for the 286 upgrade:

OX Corp. StaX/SX	(617) 890-4402
Cumulus Corp. 386SX Card	(216) 464-2211
Intel's Snap-In	(503) 629-7402
Kingston's SX Now	(714) 435-2600

Most of the modules are quite similar. Figure 3-6 shows a Kingston SX Now compare it with Figs. 3-3 and 3-4. Plugging in a processor module is about the easiest way to upgrade a 286.

Upgrading a 386DX to a 486

The Cyris Company has a 486 CPU that is pin compatible with the 386DX chip. Just remove the 386 CPU and plug in the Cyrix CPU. This chip also comes with a coprocessor that plugs into the 387 socket, providing the coprocessing ability of true 486DX systems.

The Cyrix 486 CPU operates internally at 40MHz but it can be used in any 386DX system. This upgrade proves almost all the power and functionality of a true 486DX 33MHz system. The Cyrix 486 CPU costs less than half as much as the Intel 486DX 33MHz chip. It is the easiest and least expensive way that I know of to upgrade to 486 power.

Chapter 4

Motherboards and plug-in boards

The motherboard is the largest and most important board in your system. I have included photos of several motherboards, but there are hundreds of manufacturers so your motherboard might be slightly different than those pictured. But from the lowly XT up to the powerful 486, motherboards are all basically the same. Except for the CPU, they all have the same basic components and operate the same way. Of course, the more powerful 386 and 486 systems are more complex so they have more components and circuitry.

Motherboards

In the early days, most motherboards looked very much alike. They had dozens of discrete basic chip components. Today, motherboards look different because manufacturers design them with many of the basic components combined in VLSI chips.

CPUs

The most important component on the motherboard is the CPU, such as an 80286 or 80386SX. It is a square chip and might be similar to several other VLSI chips on your motherboard. Figure 4-1 shows a 386SX chip. The CPU is the major chip and is the brains of the computer. It controls almost everything.

4-1 A 386SX CPU chip.

Differences between the various CPUs

You might have some doubts about building a 286. After all, there are a lot of computers on the market that are much faster and more powerful than the 286. For instance, the 386SX, 386DX, 486SX, and 486DX are all more powerful than the 286. But like everything else in life, if it is bigger and better, it costs more.

Intel developed the first 286. It was the CPU used in the first IBM AT. At that time, it was a very powerful and advanced CPU. Intel couldn't manufacture enough of them to fill all the orders.

Intel agreed to a license that allowed Advanced Micro Devices (AMD) to manufacture the 286. This was a decision that they later regretted very much. They still sold more 286 CPUs than AMD, but it did eat into their profits. Intel later developed the more powerful 386DX, the 386SX, the 486, and then the 486SX.

As Intel lost more of their 286 market share, they began a concerted campaign to convince manufacturers to abandon the 286. They wanted everybody to replace the 286 CPU with the 386SX. But most knowledgeable people realize that the 286 is a very good alternative for the vast majority of average computing needs, and despite Intel's efforts, the 286 is still very much alive.

Intel has still more problems. Companies such as AMD and Chips and Technology have developed 386SX and 386DX chips that are faster and use less power than Intel's. To counter this thrust, Intel is trying to get people to switch to the 486SX.

A lot of people will listen to Intel and abandon perfectly good 286 and 386SX computers to move up to 486 systems, whether they need them or not. It is a bit like people and their automobiles. There are many people who don't mind driving a 10-year-old car as long as it runs well and gets them to where they want to go. There are others who would rather walk than ride in a car that isn't the very latest and most expensive.

Differences in the 286 and 386SX

The 286 CPU has 125,000 transistors in it. It is a 16-bit device; that is, it processes data two bytes, or two words, at a time. Internally, the 386SX processes data 32 bits, or four words, at a time. But externally, it uses a 16-bit bus, the same as the 286. The 386DX and 486 systems process data 32 bits at a time. They also communicate with their memory over a 32-bit bus both internally and externally. This makes memory access and processing very fast. But the 386 and 486 systems use the same 16-bit bus that the 286 uses to communicate with plug-in boards, disk drives, and other peripherals. In this respect, the 386 and 486 might be limited to the same speed as the 286. Table 4-1 gives a short summary of the differences in the various CPUs.

Table 4-1. Differences in various CPUs

	XT	286	386SX	386DX	486
Transistors	29,000	120,000	200,000	275,000	1,200,00
Frequency	4.7–10 MHz	6–25 MHz	16–33 MHz	16–40 MHz	25–50 MHz
Bits	8	16	16 (32)	32	32
Memory addition	640 K	16Mb	32Mb	4Gb	64Gb

The higher-frequency versions of the CPU chips cost more. The prices frequently change, usually downward. One reason they are coming down is because AMD and Chips and Technology are now manufacturing 386 chips and giving Intel some competition.

Computers are a lot like automobiles. The XT can be compared to the small compact. Neither is very powerful or fast, but they are quite economical. The 286 can be compared to the lower-priced midsize cars. The 386SX can be compared to the mid-sized cars that have a few added luxuries. The 386DX and 486SX can be compared to the luxurious and very expensive top-of-the-line cars, and the 486DX can be compared to the Rolls-Royce.

Depending on your applications and what you want to do with your computer, you might not need to spend money for the extra power and speed of a 386 or 486. The 286 can run all of the programs that a 386 or 486 can run, though it is a bit slower than the 386 and 486 systems.

The 286 CPU operates at frequencies of 6 MHz to 25 MHz; the 386SX operates at 16 MHz to 33 MHz. The 386DX and 486 operate at frequencies of 40 MHz or higher. Of course, the higher the CPU frequency, the more data that can be processed in a given amount of time. For some high-end applications the higher speed is very necessary.

BIOS

Your motherboard will have BIOS chips. Some systems might have two 256K ROM chips, others might have a single 512K ROM chip. The ROM chips have a set of programs burned into the read-only memory. The primary function of the BIOS is to control and facilitate the transfer of data and control instructions between the computer, disk drives, and other peripherals.

There are several BIOS manufacturers, such as Award, Phoenix, AMI, Quadtel, and others. Each of them provide BIOS chips that are slightly different. Some include diagnostic routines in their chips. The AMI BIOS has an extensive set of routines that can check the speed of your hard and floppy drives, check the access speed, let you format your hard disk, check the disk media for bad sectors, check the operation of your keyboard, check the printer and COM ports, and several other tests.

 Most motherboard manufacturers buy the basic BIOS license from the manufacturer and customize the BIOS in some way for their particular motherboards. Thus, a BIOS taken from one motherboard might not work on a motherboard from a different manufacturer.

There is a keyboard BIOS chip, usually located near the keyboard connector, at the rear of the motherboard. Other chips control the timing circuits, the memory circuits, and related components. These chips might be integrated into VLSI chips.

CMOS

Your motherboard will have a CMOS chip that contains the system configuration. The BIOS allows you to write to the system CMOS configuration. These semiconductors draw very little power. A small rechargeable battery on the motherboard provides power to keep the CMOS circuits alive when the power is off. When you first set up your computer, the CMOS must be told such things as the type of hard drive, the type of floppies, the time, and the date. If you add a hard disk, change the time or date, or make other changes, the CMOS configuration must be changed.

Causes of incompatibility

The original IBM PCs and XTs came with BASICA, IBM's version of the BASIC programming language, in four ROM chips. The semiconductors within a ROM chip are configured and programmed for a specific purpose or task. This memory is non-volatile and cannot be written on or changed by ordinary means.

IBM would not sell these chips to anyone, so only genuine IBM PCs and XTs had BASIC ROM. With BASICA in ROM, you did not have to load it from a floppy diskette. It was quite handy and fast, almost like having a small hard disk. Several software programs were written to take advantage of IBM's BASICA ROM.

Microsoft released GW-BASIC on floppy disks for the rest of the world, but BASIC programs that were developed specifically for the IBM BASICA ROMs could not run on the clones. This was one of the greatest causes of incompatibility.

Another cause of incompatibility was IBM's BIOS chip. In order to run the same software and perform the same functions, the clone machines had to have a BIOS that was very similar to the IBM BIOS. Rather than go to the expense and trouble of developing an IBM compatible BIOS, some of the clone manufacturers just copied IBM's. This made IBM a bit unhappy and the culprits were threatened with lawsuits. Some went out of business, but several companies developed BIOS chips that were almost 100 percent compatible with IBM.

I don't know of any BIOS incompatibilities among IBM and the clones today. Incidentally, there are many more clones in existence than IBMs. So even if there are differences, who should worry about being compatible, IBM or the larger number of clones?

The original XT BIOS used a single 128K ROM chip. But the AT required more than 128K to store all of the new added functions, so two 128K chips were used. Most of the AT-type systems now use two 256K ROM chips (for a total of 512K) to hold all of the functions needed. To give you an idea of how much 512K is, all of the text in this book can be stored in less than 500K.

Refer back to Fig. 3-12, a photo of an XT and 286 motherboard. In the lower portion of the XT motherboard are eight 62-pin connectors or slots for plug-in boards. A plug-in board, such as a monitor adapter, floppy controller, or modem, can be plugged into any one of the slots. Etched lines connect each of the 62 pins on each connector or slot. For instance, all pin 1s of each slot are tied together. So are pin 2s, 3s, etc. This allows you to use any one of the eight slots for any plug-in board. These lines allow communication with the CPU, RAM, ROM, plug-in boards, disk drives, keyboard, printers, modems, faxes, and other peripherals and accessories. The data flows back and forth over these lines which is called the bus. The XT has an 8-bit bus.

The AT-type systems, which include the 286, 386, and 486, use a 16-bit bus. The 16-bit bus requires more connections, so the 286 motherboard in Fig. 3-12 has four extra 36-pin connectors in front of the eight 62-pin connectors.

RAM

If you refer back to Figs. 3-1 and 3-2, the RAM section is located on the lower right corner of the motherboard. There are four rows of sockets for plugging in the RAM ICs. There are nine sockets per row, or bank. Each chip has 8K of memory. It actually takes nine of the 8K chips to make 64K and nine 32K chips to make 256K. The ninth chip in each bank is used for parity checking and other housekeeping chores. To get 640K on the board, two of the rows of sockets are jumpered so that they will accept 256K chips. This gives a total of 512K. The other two banks are filled with standard 64K chips for 128K. When added to the 512K, this gives a total of the 640K minimum.

Most of the motherboards manufactured today have sockets for single in-line memory modules (SIMMs), or single in-line package (SIP) memory. They are more compact and require much less board space so more memory can be installed on the motherboard.

The 286 motherboard

Refer back to Fig. 2-2. It shows a standard-size AT or 286 motherboard. Because it needs extra chips and 16-bit connectors, it is larger than the XT. But there are "baby" size 286, 386, and 486 motherboards that are the same size as the XT. Their size was reduced by combining several of the chips and using VLSI technology.

The lower left portion of the 286 motherboard has the plug-in slots. It has eight 62-pin slots just like the XT, but it also has six extra 36-pin slots in front of the 62-pin slots. These 36-pin slots enable the 286 to process data 16 bits at a time, twice as much as the XT. Remember that it takes eight bits to create a single character or numeral. These eight bits, or one byte, are considered to be one word. The 16-bit 286 is considered to be a two-word machine, the 32-bit 386 and 486 are four-word machines.

The 286 CPU is the square, white object in the center of the board. The 80286 CPU has 125,000 transistors, so it is considerably more complex than the 8088. The fastest XT operates at about 12 MHz, the 286 can operate as high as 25 MHz. Compared to the XT, the 286 can process up to four times the amount of data in the same length of time. The XT only has 20 address lines so it is limited to 1Mb of memory (two states—on and off—is 2^{20}, or 1,048,576 bytes, which is called 1Mb). The 286 has 24 address lines and can address 16Mb (2^{24} is 16,777,216 bytes).

The 286 can also operate in the protected mode and is able to run more than one program at a time (multitasking). It can load and run two or more programs into RAM and process them at the same time. The protected mode puts a wall around each application and keeps them from interfering with one another. I will present more about the protected mode in chapter 13 when I discuss Windows.

The 286 memory chips are in the lower right corner, the same general location as in the XT. Most newer motherboards use SIMMs or SIP memory, which allows a higher memory density. Several megabytes can be installed in the same area that 640K would occupy on an older motherboard.

Cost

The cost of the 286 motherboard depends on the CPU frequency, the amount of installed memory, and the built-in functions. They might cost $70 to $125. Depending on your computing requirements, a 286 might be all you need.

The 386SX motherboard

The 386SX CPU is a scaled-down version of the 386DX. It has 200,000 transistors. It has 24 external lines so it can address 16Mb, just like the 286. Again like the 286, the 386SX communicates with its on-board RAM, plug-in boards, and peripherals over 16-bit bus lines. Once the data reaches the CPU, it is processed at a rate of 32 bits. The 286 and 386SX can both operate at 25 MHz, but the 386SX processes data twice as fast. The 386SX also makes better use of the protected mode, and with the proper software, can run in the 386 enhanced mode. This mode allows the computer to set aside a portion of the hard disk and use it as virtual memory. Figure 4-2 shows a 386SX motherboard that can operate at 25 MHz or 33 MHz.

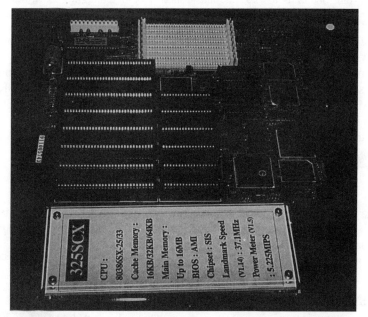

4-2 A 386SX motherboard that can operate at 25 MHz or 33 MHz.

Figure 4-3 shows a 386SX motherboard that was designed for the low-profile type of system. The case is not high enough to accommodate standard boards plugged in vertically. There is a single 16-bit slot for a daughterboard with five slots. Three boards can be mounted horizontally on one side of the daughterboard and two on the

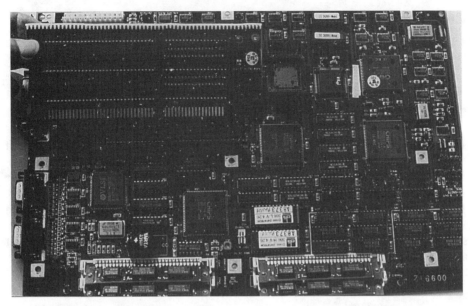

4-3 A low-profile 386SX motherboard. It has a single slot for a daughterboard with five slots.

other. It is very cramped and it is impossible to mount five standard-size boards. You would have to use half-size boards on the disk drive side.

This motherboard, from DTK, has a built-in IDE interface that can control two hard disks. It also has a built-in floppy controller that can control 360K, 720K, 1.2Mb, and 1.44Mb drives. It has a built-in parallel printer port, two serial ports, and a built-in mouse interface. The only other board needed to make a complete system is a monitor adapter. It can accept up to 4Mb of SIMM DRAM (dynamic RAM) using 1Mb chips or up to 16Mb using 4Mb chips.

Cost

Intel sells the 386SX CPU for about one-fourth of what they charge for the 386DX. The 16-bit bus reduces the cost of manufacturing a 586SX motherboard. The 386SX motherboard sells for $100 to $300. Because prices come down almost daily, the prices should be much lower by the time you read this.

Cache systems

When an application is processed, the program is loaded into RAM. Many programs have several loops where they use a portion of the program, then another portion, then call the first portion again, over and over. Each time a portion of a program is used, the CPU must run over to the RAM, find the address, fetch the block that it needs, go back to the CPU, and process it. The DRAMs have to be constantly refreshed, so even with very fast RAM, the CPU might have to wait a few nanoseconds. The computer might spend up to 10 percent of its time just refreshing the RAM.

The most frequently used portion of a program can be loaded in a cache, a small amount of very fast static RAM (SRAM). SRAM does not have to be refreshed so the CPU does not have to sit and wait for data. SRAM is rather expensive. If you expect to use your computer for large spreadsheets, or other memory-intensive programs, you might consider looking for a motherboard with a cache.

Cache motherboards cost from $50 to $100 more. The board might have sockets for 32K to 256K of SRAM. Of course, the more SRAM that is installed, the more it will cost.

Cache systems are usually built into the high-end 386DX and 486 systems. Only a few 386SX motherboards offer it, and it is not normally built into 286 system motherboards. Motherboard cache systems should not be confused with disk cache systems.

Local bus

The 386DX, the 486SX, and the 486DX systems process data 32 bits at a time and communicate with memory over a 32-bit bus. But all of the ISA systems, communicate with their plug-in boards and other I/O peripherals over a 16-bit bus the same as the 286 systems.

Some companies have developed what they call *local bus* ISA motherboards that have one or more slots with a 32-bit bus. One or more of the motherboard's standard 16-bit slots have an additional special slot for the 32-bit bus. At this time, there aren't many boards available for this system. Most of the boards that can use the 32-bit Local Bus are Enhanced VGA cards.

The Microlink Company (818 330-9599) offers a motherboard with one local bus slot and one EISA slot. The motherboard with a 33MHz CPU lists for $595. The enhanced VGA card for the local bus costs $340. The Syncomp Company (800-875-9799) has several different local bus motherboards. Several other companies also have them. Look for their ads in computer magazines.

Currently, there are no standards for the local bus, so not many companies are manufacturing these systems. But committees are busy hammering out a set of standards that will be acceptable to the industry. By the time you read this, the standards should be in place. The local bus only adds $25 to $50 to the manufacturing cost, but adds a tremendous amount of utility to the system. Almost all 386 and 486 motherboards will soon have the local bus.

The advancing technology

Computer technology continues to grow and expand at a dizzying pace. At this very moment, engineers and programmers are developing and designing hardware and software that will require even more memory and capabilities than we have today. The more powerful 586 will probably be out by the time you read this. Much of the fantastic technology that we have today will be obsolete tomorrow. But that doesn't mean that today's software and hardware won't still be useful tomorrow. There are many people who are still using 64K CP/M machines and running WordStar 3.0, dBASE II, and many other older programs. After all, if it satisfies the need, that is all that matters.

Chapter 5

Memory and multifunction boards

The computer uses two types of memory, random-access memory (RAM) and read-only memory (ROM). ROM is unlike RAM in several respects. ROM is fixed, permanent memory. It is like a book, it can only be read. RAM is like a blackboard, it can be written on and then erased. RAM is volatile, that is, once the power is turned off or interrupted, even for a fraction of a second, it loses all memory and any data is gone forever.

RAM and ROM

Programs and files are loaded into RAM while they are being edited or changed, or while a program is running. RAM is one of the most critical elements of the computer. If you open a file from a hard disk, the files and data are read from the disk and placed in RAM. When you load in a program, be it word processing, a spreadsheet, a database or whatever, you will be working in the system RAM. If you are writing, programming, or creating another program, you will also be working in RAM.

Being able to randomly access the computer's memory allows you to read and write to it. Here, you can manipulate data, do calculations, enter more data, edit, search databases, or do any of the thousands of things that software programs allow you to do. You can access and change the data in RAM very quickly. For most applications, the program is loaded into the standard 640K of RAM.

In addition to the application programs that must be loaded into RAM, there are certain DOS programs that must be in RAM at all times. These are programs such as Command.Com and its internal commands. There are more than 20 internal commands such as COPY, CD, CLS, DATE, DEL, MD, PATH, TIME, TYPE, and others. These commands are loaded into RAM when you boot up and are always immediately available. The Config.Sys file and any drivers that you might have for your system are also loaded into RAM.

Terminate and stay resident (TSR) files are loaded into RAM. They are memory-resident programs (like SideKick Plus and others) that can pop up anytime you press a key. Portions of RAM can also be used for a very fast RAM disk, for buffers, and for print spooling.

All of these things contribute to the utility and functionality of the computer and make it easier to use. Unfortunately, they often take big bites out of your precious 640K of RAM. There might be less than 400K left for running applications after loading all these memory-resident programs. Many programs are now so large that they won't fit in less than 600K of RAM.

DR-DOS 6.0 from Digital Research and MS-DOS 5.0 from Microsoft can now load much of the operating system and TSRs in upper memory. Upper memory is that 384K of memory above 640K (see Fig. 5-3) reserved for such functions as accessing the BIOS ROM, VRAM (video RAM), and expanded memory.

Several memory management programs have been developed to make more of the conventional 640K available for use. One excellent program is DESQview from Quarterdeck Office Systems. DESQview searches through the upper 384K of memory for any space that is not being used. It then makes this area available for loading

5-1 SIMM. The module on top is 1Mb; the one on the bottom is 512K.

TSRs, drivers, and other utilities. DESQview can even move the BIOS ROM area into expanded memory and pull it back only when it is needed. With DESQview, as much as 620K of memory can be made available for running standard programs.

A brief explanation of memory

Computers operate on binary systems of 0s and 1s (off and on). A transistor is turned off or on to represent 0 or 1. Two transistors can represent four different combinations: both off; both on; one on, one off; or one off, one on. A bank of four transistors can represent 16 different combinations. With eight transistors, there are 256 different combinations. It takes eight transistors to make one byte. With these transistors you can represent each letter of the alphabet and each number and symbol of the extended American Standard Code for Information Interchange (ASCII). With eight lines, plus a ground, the eight transistors can be turned on or off to represent any one of the 256 characters of the ASCII code.

Each byte of memory has a separate address. It is laid out similar to a large hotel's "pigeon holes" for room keys. There are horizontal rows of holes for the keys to the rooms on each floor and columns for each room. If the hotel had 100 rooms, there would be 10 horizontal rows across and 10 columns down. This matrix makes it very simple to find any one of the 100 keys by counting across and then down to the particular room number.

One megabyte of memory requires many more pigeon holes or cells. But with just 20 address lines and one ground line, any individual byte can be quickly accessed.

Dynamic RAM

Dynamic RAM, or DRAM, is the most common type of memory. It is made up of small cells similar to small capacitors. A capacitor is made from two conductive plates placed close together. When an electric charge is placed on the plates, a positive voltage on one plate and a negative voltage on the other, it acts like a battery. The capacitor retains the charge for a certain amount of time, depending on the area of the conductors and certain other factors.

When a DRAM cell has a charge on it, it represents a 1, and when not charged, a 0. As soon as a cell is charged, it starts leaking and soon becomes discharged. The computer must go back and recharge or refresh all of the cells that are supposed to be 1s. This refreshing might take up to 7 percent of a computer's time. DRAM is relatively inexpensive and large amounts can be packed onto small chips. It is the memory of choice on almost all systems.

Refreshment and wait states

During the time that DRAM cells are being refreshed, they cannot be accessed by programs. After they have been accessed, they must be refreshed before they can be accessed again. If the CPU is operating at a very high frequency, it might have to sit and wait one cycle, or one wait state, for the refresh cycle. The wait state might be only one-millionth of a second or less. That might not seem like much time, but if the computer is doing several million operations per second, it can add up.

It takes a finite amount of time to charge the DRAM. Some DRAM can be charged much faster than others. For instance, the DRAM chips needed for an XT at 4.77 MHz might take 200 nanoseconds (ns) to be refreshed. A 386 running at 25 MHz needs chips that can be refreshed in 70 ns or less. Of course, the faster chips cost more.

Interleaved memory

Some system's memory is divided in half. Half of the memory is refreshed on one cycle; the other half on the next cycle. If the CPU needs to access an address that is in the half already refreshed, it is available immediately. This reduces the amount of waiting by half.

Cache memory

Another memory scheme to speed up refreshing is to install a small amount of very fast DRAM or SRAM in a cache near the CPU. A cache system can speed up operations quite a lot. The computer can be slowed down considerably if it has to search the entire memory each time it has to fetch some data. The data used most frequently can be stored in the fast cache memory, increasing the speed by several magnitudes.

The cache might be from 64K to 256K or more. When running an application program, the CPU often loops in and out of certain areas, repeatedly using the same memory. If this often-used memory is stored in the cache, it can be accessed by the CPU quicker.

You can't arbitrarily add cache to a system. The motherboard usually has to be designed for it. If you are going to need a very fast system, you should look for a motherboard that has a cache on it. Most cache motherboards are designed for the 386DX and 486. There are only a few 386SX cache motherboards.

Cache memory should not be confused with disk caching. Often, a program might need to access a hard disk while running. If a small disk cache is set up in RAM, the program will run much faster.

Static RAM

Static RAM, or SRAM, is made up of actual transistors that can be turned on to represent 1s or left off to represent 0s, and they will stay in that condition until receiving a change signal. SRAM transistors need not be refreshed, but they revert back to 0 when the computer is turned off or if the power is interrupted. They are very fast and can operate at speeds of 25 ns or less.

A DRAM cell needs only one transistor and a small capacitor. Each SRAM cell requires four to six transistors and other components. Besides being more expensive, SRAM chips are physically larger and require more space than DRAM chips. Because of the physical and electronic differences, SRAM and DRAM chips are not interchangeable. The motherboard must be designed for SRAM.

Many laptops use SRAM because it can be kept alive with a small amount of current from a battery. Because DRAM needs to be constantly refreshed, it takes a lot of circuitry and power to keep it alive.

The cost of SRAM is coming down. I bought a Toshiba laptop in 1989 and added 2Mb of SRAM on a cartridge. It cost $900, or about the same as the original price of the entire laptop. Today, that same 2Mb SRAM cartridge costs about $150.

Flash memory

Intel has developed flash memory, which is similar to eraseable programmable read-only memory (EPROM). Flash memory on small, plug-in cards is about the size of a credit card. It is available on some small palm-size computers, such as the PSIONs. Flash memory is still rather expensive, but several foreign companies have begun development along the same lines. A Personal Computer Card International Association standard has been proposed that would make the cards interchangeable among various laptops.

Motherboard memory

The XT motherboard can accept 640K of memory. The 286 and 386SX can accept up to 16Mb on the motherboard.

Bus systems

The XT communicates with its plug-in boards and memory chips, eight data bits at a time. Etched copper lines physically connect each plug-in socket and the motherboard memory chips. This is called the *bus*. The 286 and 386SX are 16-bit systems and the motherboards use a 16-bit bus. Because both memory and the bus are 16 bit, there is no degradation of speed when using a plug-in memory board.

If your motherboard does not provide sockets for the memory that you want, there are several companies that make memory plug-in boards. Some of these boards have SIMM connectors that will accept up to 32Mb of DRAM.

The 386DX and 486 have 32-bit memory systems and a 32-bit bus to communicate with memory, but they use a 16-bit bus to communicate with the plug-in boards. A plug-in memory board on a 32-bit system will slow it down because of the 16-bit bus.

Single inline memory module

Your computer motherboard will probably have sockets for single inline memory modules, or SIMMs. A SIMM is an assembly of miniature DRAM chips. Usually nine chips on a small board are plugged into a special connector. SIMMs require a very small amount of space (see Fig. 5-1). The module on top has 1Mb, the one below has 512K).

Single inline package

Some motherboards might have single inline packages, or SIP memory. A SIP is similar to a SIMM except that it has pins (see Fig. 5-2). Each module is 1Mb at a speed of 70 ns.

Currently, 1Mb DRAM chips are the largest available. You should be able to buy 4Mb chips by the time you read this and 16Mb chips will soon be available. Some companies are working on 64Mb DRAM chips, but it will be some time before they get to market.

5-2 SIP. Each module is 1Mb at 70 ns.

If you plan to add extra memory, be sure that you get the right type for your machine. Make sure that it is fast enough for your system. Check your documentation; it should tell you what speed and type of chips to buy.

How much memory do you need?

How much memory you need depends on what you intend to use your computer for. When you run a program, data is read from the disk into RAM and is operated on there. You can get by with 640K for word processing or small applications. You should have at least 4Mb if you expect to use Windows, large databases, or spreadsheets.

Having lots of memory is like having a car with a large engine. You might not need that extra power very often, but it sure feels great being able to call on it when you do need it.

Types of memory

Conventional memory

Conventional memory is the 1Mb of memory that includes the 640K (see Fig. 5-3). The 384K of memory above 640K is reserved for video, ROM BIOS, and other functions.

Extended memory

Extended memory is memory that can be installed above 1Mb (see Fig. 5-3). If it weren't for the 640K limitation of DOS, it would be a seamless continuation of memory. Windows 3.0 and several other software applications will let 286 and larger computers use this memory.

```
4Gb

              Extended memory


1024K     Conventional memory

              ROM BIOS
              256K reserved

           Expanded memory
              Page frame

                 Video
           128K reserved space

640K


                 RAM
           for DOS and applications
                 programs


OK
```

```
           Expanded memory
              up to 32Mb

           Usable by DOS
          applications adhering
           to LIM specifications
```

5-3 Memory arrangement.

Expanded memory

Some large spreadsheets require an enormous amount of memory. A few years ago in a rare instance of cooperation among corporations, Lotus, Intel, Microsoft, and some other large corporations got together and devised a system and standard specification called LIM EMS (Lotus-Intel-Microsoft expanded memory specification) 4.0. It allows a computer, even a PC or XT, to address up to 32Mb of expanded memory. The memory is divided into pages of 16K each. Expanded memory finds a 64K window that is not being used above the 640K of the 1Mb conventional memory (see Fig. 5-3). Pages of 16K expanded memory are switched in and out of this window.

LIM EMS also includes functions for multitasking so that several programs can be run simultaneously. The system can treat extra memory on the 286, 386, and 486 as extended memory with the proper software and drivers.

Memory modes

There are three different memory modes: real, standard or protected, and 386 enhanced.

Real mode

Real mode memory is the mode that most of us have been using until now. When an application is processed, the program is loaded into RAM. The CPU uses the RAM to process any data that is input. Computations, changes, or calculations are done in memory, then sent back to the disk, screen, printer, or other device. For most single-user applications, this processing is done in the standard 640K or less of RAM.

Breaking the 640K barrier with LIM EMS

LIM EMS was designed to solve the 640K barrier problem. Expanded memory can be accessed, a small amount at a time, through memory above 640K. Expanded memory is like adding an extra room onto a building. When the building is full, you can store extra material in the added room. But to use the extra material, you have to go through a door and move a small amount at a time.

The LIM EMS scheme allows up to 32Mb of expanded memory to be added to a system. But it can only be accessed through a small window above 640K. Only 64K of data can be moved in or out of the window at a time. The LIM EMS systems works on the XT, as well as larger AT-type machines.

Windows 3.1   With Windows 3.1, there is not as much need for LIM EMS on AT-type machines. Windows 3.1 lets you go beyond the 640K barrier, lets you do multitasking, and lets you take advantage of the virtual and protected modes. It works with a mouse and icons and can make your PC easier to use than a Macintosh. Windows is also relatively inexpensive.

DESQview   DESQview also allows you to break through the 640K barrier. DESQview is an excellent, inexpensive program that takes advantage of the 486's virtual 8086 and 32-bit protected mode. It allows you to run multiple DOS programs simultaneously, switch between them, run programs in the background, and transfer data between them.

Standard or protected mode

XTs can only address 1Mb. This 1Mb is 640K of lower memory and 384K of upper memory. The ROM BIOS and video usually do not require all of the reserved 384K, so portions of it can be used to access expanded memory.

The 286, 386, and 486 are also limited to 640K in the real mode. With the proper software, however, the 286 can address 16Mb and the 386 can address 4Gb. With Windows 3.1 and the proper application software, you can use extended memory on a 286, 386SX, 386, or 486.

In the protected mode, with the proper software applications, you can also load two or more programs into memory and process both of them at the same time. If you tried this in real mode, the data from both programs would be all mixed together. The data from both programs is just 0s and 1s. If you mix them together, it's like mixing a gallon of hot water with a gallon of cold water. The CPUs of the 286, 386, and 486 have a built-in system that can put a "wall" around 1Mb of RAM and let it work just as if it were a separate 8086 computer. Essentially, you have several 8086 computers working on different applications at the same time.

The 386 enhanced mode

With the proper software applications, the 386SX, the 386DX, and 486 can use all of the extended memory available. They will also set aside a portion of your hard disk and use it as virtual memory. This allows programs of 32Mb or more to be processed at one time. The 286 cannot operate in this mode, but it can do just about everything else the 386 can do.

Chapter 6

Floppy drives and disks

It is possible to run a computer with just a floppy drive. My first computer had two single-sided 140K drives. It was slow and required a lot of disk swapping. Floppy systems have come a long way since those early days. The 140K systems were soon replaced with 320K double-sided systems, then 360K, 1.2Mb, 1.44Mb, 2.88Mb, and now even 21Mb on a floppy disk.

Floppy drives

Floppy disks and floppy drives are a very important part of your computer. The majority of all software programs come to us on floppy drives. The software is then copied from the floppy disks to a hard disk. Floppy disks are also needed to archive programs and back up your hard disk.

There are about 40 million 360K drives still in use, so most programs are still distributed on 360K disks. The old 360K format has served us well, but it is now obsolete. The 5¼-inch 1.2Mb drive can read and write to the 360K format as well as the high-density format.

The 3½-inch 1.44Mb drive can read and write to the 720K format as well as the high-density format. The 720K drive is also obsolete.

Although both the 360K and 720K drives are obsolete, many vendors are still advertising and selling them for about the same price as the high-density drives. I recommend that you buy 1.2Mb or 1.44Mb drives. Or better yet, buy both of them. You will then be covered for all formats.

Many computers only provide three or four bays to mount drives. You might not have space to mount two floppies, two hard drives, a tape backup drive, and a CD-ROM. The CMS Enhancements Company noted this problem. They created an all-media floppy drive by combining a 1.2Mb and 1.44Mb floppy drive in a single unit (see Fig. 6-1). This allows both drives to be installed in a single drive bay. The two drives are never used at the same time, so there is no problem. They can even share some of the drive electronics.

How floppy disk drives operate

The floppy drive spins a disk much like a record player. The floppy disk is made from a type of plastic material called polyethylene terephthalate. This is coated with a magnetic material made primarily of iron oxide. Basically it is similar to the tape used in cassette tape recorders. The drive uses a head that records (writes) and plays back (reads) the disk much like the record/playback head in a cassette recorder. When the head writes or records on the iron oxide surface, a pulse of electricity causes the head to magnetize that portion of the track beneath the head. When the tracks are read, the head detects whether each portion of the track is magnetized or not. If the spot is magnetized, it creates a small voltage signal representing a 1 (or a 0 if it is not magnetized).

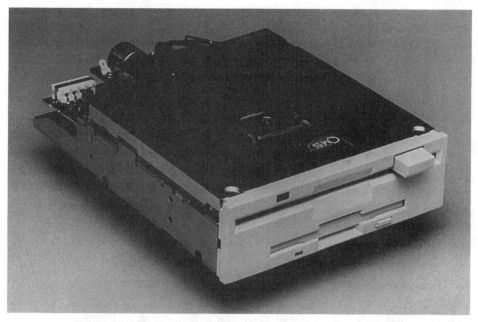

6-1 A CMS all-media floppy drive for both 5¼-inch and 3½-inch floppies.

Types of disks

The 5¼-inch 360K and the 3½-inch 720K disks are called *double sided, double density* (DS/DD). The 5¼-inch 1.2Mb and the 3½-inch 1.44Mb disks are called high density (HD). The 3½-inch double-density disks are usually marked DD, the high-density disks are usually marked HD. But the 5¼-inch 360K and 1.2Mb disks usually have no markings. They look exactly alike, except that the 360K disks usually have a reinforcing ring or collar around the large center hole. The high-density 1.2Mb disks do not have this ring.

One of the major differences between 720K and 1.44Mb disks is that the high-density 1.44Mb disks have two small square holes at the rear of the plastic shell, while 720K disks have only one hole. Compare the disks in Fig. 6-2. The one on the left is 1.44Mb, the one on the right is 720K.

The hole on the right rear of the shell has a small slide that can be moved to cover the hole. A microswitch on the drive checks the hole when the disk is inserted. If the hole is covered, then the disk can be written on. If it is open, then the disk is write-protected. The 3½-inch disk's write-protect system is just the opposite of the system used by the 5¼-inch disks. The square notch must be covered with opaque tape to prevent writing on or unintentional erasing of the disk. Incidentally, you must use opaque tape. The 5¼-inch system uses a light that shines through the square notch. If the detector in the system can see the light through the notch, then it can write on the disk. Some people have used transparent tape to cover the notch, with disastrous results.

6-2 A high-density 1.44Mb disk (left) and a 720K disk (right).

On most of the 1.44Mb 3½-inch drives there is a microswitch that checks for the hole on the right rear of the disk. If you insert a disk and the drive finds a hole in the right rear it will allow you to format, read, and write the disk as 1.44Mb.

Disk format structure

Tracks

A disk must be formatted before it can be used. This consists of laying out individual concentric tracks on each side of the disk. If it is a 360K disk, each side is marked or configured with 40 tracks, numbered from 0 to 39. Figure 6-3 shows a 360K disk that has been opened up and marked to represent tracks and sectors.

If it is a 1.2Mb, 720K, or 1.44Mb disk, each side is configured with 80 tracks, numbered from 0 to 79 (see Table 6-1). The tracks have the same number on the top and bottom of the disk. The top is side 0 and the bottom is side 1. When the head is over track 1 on the top, it is also over track 1 on the bottom. The heads move as a single unit to the various tracks using a head positioner. When data is written to a track, as much as possible is written on the top track, then the head is electronically switched and it continues to write to the same track on the bottom side. It is much faster and easier to switch between the heads than to move them to another track.

Cylinders

If you could strip away all of the other tracks on each side of track 1 on side 0 and track 1 on side 1, it would be very flat but might resemble a cylinder. Two heads read and write on the disk, head 0 on the top and head 1 on the bottom. When head 0 is over track 1, sector 1, on the top of the disk, head 1 is addressing track 1, sector 1 on the bottom of the disk. The heads move from track to track as a single unit. Data is written to track 1 on the top side, then the heads are electronically switched to the bottom side and writing is continued to track 1 on the bottom side.

6-3 An open floppy diskette. Markings on the diskette represent tracks and sectors.

Sectors

Each of the tracks are divided into sectors: 360K into 9 sectors, 1.2Mb into 15 sectors, 720K into 9 sectors, 1.44Mb into 18 sectors, and 2.88Mb into 36 sectors (see Table 6-1). Each sector can contain 512 bytes. Multiplying the number of sectors times number of bytes per sector times the number of tracks times two sides gives the amount of data that can be stored on a disk. For instance the 1.2Mb disk has 15 sectors times 512 bytes times 80 tracks times 2 sides ($15 \times 512 \times 80 \times 2 = 1,228,800$ bytes). The system uses 14,898 bytes to mark the tracks and sectors during formatting, so there is actually 1,213,902 bytes available on a 1.2Mb floppy.

Clusters or allocation units

DOS allocates one or more sectors on a disk and calls it a cluster or allocation unit. On 360K and 720K disks, a cluster or allocation unit is two sectors. On the 1.2Mb and 1.44Mb disks, each allocation unit is one sector. Only single files or parts of single files can be written into an allocation unit. If two different files were written into a single allocation unit, the data would become mixed and corrupted.

File allocation table

During formatting, a file allocation table (FAT) is created on the first track of the disk. This FAT acts like a table of contents for a book. Whenever a file is recorded on a disk, the file is broken up into allocation units. The head looks at the FAT to find

Table 6-1. Capacities of various disk types.

Disk type	Tracks per side	Sectors per track	Unformatted capacity	System use	Available to user	Maximum directories
360K	40	9	368,640	6144	362,496	112
1.2Mb	80	15	1,228,800	14,898	1,213,992	224
3½′	80	9	737,280	12,800	724,480	224
3½′	80	18	1,474,560	16,896	1,457,664	224
3½′	80	36	2,949,120		2.88Mb	224

empty units, then records the parts of the file in any empty units it can find. Part of the file might be recorded in sector 5 of track 10, part in sector 8 of track 15, and any place it can find empty sectors. It records the location of all the various parts of the file in the FAT. With this method, parts of a file can be erased, changed, or added to without changing the entire disk.

TPI

The 40 tracks of a 360K disk are laid down at a rate of 48 tracks per inch (TPI), so each of the 40 tracks is ⅟₄₈ inch wide. The 80 tracks of the high-density 1.2Mb disk are laid down at a rate of 96 TPI, so each track is ⅟₉₆ inch wide. The 80 tracks of a 1.44Mb disk are laid down at a density of 135 TPI, or ⅟₁₃₅ inch per track.

Read accuracy

The 5¼-inch disks have a 1⅛-inch center hole. The drives have a conical spindle that comes up through the hole when the drive latch is closed. This centers the disk so that the heads are able to find each track. The plastic material that the disk is made from is subject to environmental changes and wear and tear. The conical spindle might not center each disk exactly, so head-to-track accuracy is difficult with more than 80 tracks. Most of the 360K disks use a reinforcing ring, but it probably doesn't help much. The 1.2Mb floppies do not use a hub ring. Except for the hub ring, the 360K and 1.2Mb disks look exactly the same.

The tracks of the 3½-inch floppies are narrower and greater in density per inch. But because of the metal hub, the head-tracking accuracy is much better than that of the 5¼-inch systems.

Hard disks have very accurate head-tracking systems. Some have a density of more than 1000 TPI, so much more data can be stored on a hard disk.

Rotation speed

Floppy disks have a very smooth lubricated surface. They rotate at a fairly slow 300 rpm. Magnetic lines of force deteriorate very fast with distance. So, the closer the heads, the better they can read and write. The heads directly contact the floppy disks.

Hard disks rotate at 3600 rpm. The heads and surface would be severely damaged if they came in contact at this speed. The heads "fly" over the surface a few millionths of an inch above it.

Differences in disks

There are about 70 million PCs in use. More than half of them have the old 360K drives. Most software companies still distribute software on 360K disks because almost everybody can read that format. What is really fantastic is that the 1.2Mb drives can also read and write to the 360K format.

The 360K and 1.2Mb disks look exactly alike except for the hub ring on the 360K disks. But there is a great difference in their magnetic materials, which determines the oersted (Oe) of each one. The Oe is a measure of the resistance of a material to being magnetized. The lower the Oe, the easier the material is magnetized. The 360K disks have an Oe of 300, while 1.2Mb disks have an Oe of 600. The 360K disks are fairly easy to write to and require a fairly low head current. The 1.2Mb disks are more difficult to magnetize so a much higher head current is required. This current is switched to match whatever type of disk you tell the system you are using.

It is possible to format a 360K disk as a 1.2Mb disk, but several bad sectors will be found, especially near the center where the sectors are shorter. These sectors will be marked and locked out. The system might report that you have over 1Mb of space on a 360K disk. I do not recommend that you use such a disk for any data that is important. The data might eventually deteriorate and become unusable.

The 3½-inch drives have several good features. The 720K disks can store twice as much data as the 360K disks, and the 1.44Mb can store four times more in a smaller space. They have a hard plastic protective shell, so they are not easily damaged. They also have a spring-loaded shutter that automatically covers and protects the head opening when the disk is not in use.

Another feature is the write-protect system. A plastic slide can be moved to open or close a small square hole in the shell. When the slide covers the opening, the disk is write-enabled. When the slide is moved to open the square hole, it is write-protected. This system of write protection is exactly the opposite of that used in the 5¼-inch system.

If the square notch on the 5¼-inch system is left uncovered, light can shine through, allowing the disk to be written to or erased. If the notch is covered with opaque tape, the disk can only be read. Do not use clear tape. The system depends on a light shining through the notch, and if clear tape is used, the disk can be written on or erased.

In Fig. 6-2, the disk on the left is a 1.44Mb and is marked MFD-2HD (micro floppy disk, the 2 means double-sided, the HD is for high density). The disk on the right is marked MFD-2DD (micro floppy disk, double-sided, double density). Note the arrows at the top left corner of the disks indicating how they should be inserted into the drive. Because of their design, they cannot be completely inserted into a drive upside down or backwards, so no damage can be done.

Formatting

To format a 360K disk with the 1.2Mb drive, assuming that the 1.2Mb drive is the A drive, type FORMAT A/4. To format to 1.2Mb, you need high-density disks. If the system is configured and the controller allows it, you only have to type FORMAT A:. If you insert a 360K disk, the drive will try to format it to 1.2Mb and several bad sectors will probably be found.

To format a 720K disk on a 1.44Mb drive, type FORMAT B: /T:80 /N:9. To format a 1.44Mb disk, just type FORMAT B: (you might have to type FORMAT B: /T:80 /N:18).

Format .bat files

Here are some batch files that save me much time when formatting disks:

```
COPY CON FM36.BAT
C FORMAT A: /4
^Z

COPY CON FM12.BAT
C: FORMAT A: /T:80 /N:15
^Z

COPY CON FM72.BAT
C: FORMAT B: /T:80 /N:9
^Z

COPY CON FM14.BAT
C: FORMAT B: /T:80 /N:18
^Z
```

The ^Z is made by pressing F6. With these batch files, I only have to type fm36 for a 360K disk, fm12 for a 1.2Mb disk, fm72 for a 720K disk, or fm14 for a 1.44Mb disk. These .bat files apply to DR-DOS 6.0 and versions of MS-DOS through version 4.01

MS-DOS 5.0 will also format a 360K disk in a high-density drive, but the command has been changed. A switch has been added that can be invoked with the for command. It eliminates the need to type in parameters for the various formats. To format a 360K disk, type FORMAT A:/f:360, for a 1.2Mb, type FORMAT A:/f:1.2, for a 720K, type FORMAT B:/f:720, and for a 1.44Mb, type FORMAT B:/f:1.44. All of these commands can be considerably shortened if made into .bat files similar to those above.

If you try to reformat a previously formatted disk with MS-DOS 5.0, it will try to format it the same way. For instance, if you made a mistake and formatted a 360K disk as a 1.2Mb disk, MS-DOS 5.0 will format it as a 1.2Mb disk if you don't use the /f:360 switch.

Disk costs

The cost of all floppy disks are now quite reasonable. The 360K DS/DD disks are selling for as low as 21 cents each, and the 720K disks are going for as little as 35 cents each. The 1.2Mb HD disks are selling at discount houses for as little as 39 cents each, and the 1.44Mb HD disks are selling for as little as 59 cents each.

These are real bargains. You can buy 10 of the 1.44Mb disks or 14.4Mb of storage for $5.90. This is less than 25 cents per megabyte. You can buy 10 of the 1.2Mb disks for only $3.90. You can store 12Mb of data on them at a cost of less than 31 cents per megabyte. If you use a good compression backup software, such as Norton Utilities or Fastback Plus, you can store more than 28Mb on 10 1.44Mb disks, or about 24Mb on 10 1.2Mb disks.

Discount disk sources

Here are just a few companies that sell disks at a discount. There are several others. Check the computer magazines for ads.

- MEI/Micro Center   (800) 634-3478
- The Disk Barn   (800) 727-3475
- Americal Group   (800) 288-8025
- MidWest Micro   (800) 423-8215

Floppy controllers

A floppy disk must have a controller. In the early days, a controller was a separate board full of chips. Today, it is usually built into a single VLSI chip that is integrated with a hard disk controller or IDE interface. It might also be integrated with a multi-function board or built-in on the motherboard.

Higher-density systems

Floppy technology continues to advance and several new higher-capacity drives and disks are now available.

Extended density (ED) drives

Several companies are now offering a 3½-inch extended density 2.8Mb floppy drive. The 2.8Mb disks have a barium ferrite media and use perpendicular recording to achieve the extended density. In standard recording, the particles are magnetized so that they lay horizontally in the media. In perpendicular recording, the particles are stood vertically on end for greater density.

The ED drives are downward compatible and can read and write to 720K and 1.44Mb disks. Currently, ED drives are still rather expensive. IBM has announced that they will use them on one of their PS/2 units, and no doubt, they will become the new standard. By the time you read this, they should be reasonably priced.

Very high density drives

Brier Technology and Insite have developed 3½-inch drives that can store over 20Mb on a disk. There is no standard among the competing systems, so they use different methods to achieve their very high density.

One of the problems that had to be overcome in very high density drives was that of tracking. The drives have little trouble reading and writing to the 135 TPI of the standard 3½-inch disk. But 20Mb requires many more tracks that are much closer together. Brier Technology's Flextra uses special disks that have special magnetic servo tracks embedded beneath the data tracks.

The Insite disks have optical servo tracks that are etched into the surface with a laser beam. The heads then lock onto the servo tracks for accurate reading and writing to the data tracks. The Insite drive has a head with two different gaps. This allows it to read and write to the 20Mb format as well as the 720K and 1.44Mb formats.

The Brier Technology drive is being distributed by the Q'COR Company. The special disks for these systems cost about $20 each. Figure 6-4 shows a couple of Brier external QuadFlextra drives along with 3½-inch floppy disks.

6-4 The QuadFlextra's high-density floppy system from Brier.

Bernoulli drives

Iomega has a high-capacity Bernoulli floppy disk system that allows the recording of up to 90Mb on a special floppy disk. The Bernoulli disk spins much faster than a standard floppy, forcing the flexible disk to bend around the heads without actually touching them. This is in accordance with the principle discovered by the Swiss scientist, Jakob Bernoulli (1654–1705).

The average seek time for the Bernoulli systems is 32 milliseconds (ms). The better hard drives have seek times of about 15 ms. The Bernoulli disks are ideal for data that might be confidential. Each person in an office might have their own 90Mb floppy that can be removed and locked up. This system is also great for backing up a hard disk system.

Iomega has dominated the very high density drive field for several years. The Bernoulli box costs about $750 for a drive and about $100 for each disk. Compression software from Stac, add Stor, and others can be used on Brier or Insite disks to store 40Mb on a 3½-inch disk. The 10Mb can double the 90Mb and store 180Mb on a 5¼-inch floppy disk.

What to buy

Many vendors are still advertising and selling 360K and 720K drives. I don't know why anyone should buy one. They are obsolete. I recommend the 1.2Mb and 1.44Mb drives, or the extended density 2.88Mb drives.

If you live near a large city, there should be lots of stores nearby, as well as computer shows and swap meets. If you don't live near a good source, then your best bet would be a mail-order house. There are lots of computer magazines that are full of ads.

Chapter 7

Hard disks

If you are completely new to computing, a hard drive is an assembly of platters with a magnetic plating. Depending on the capacity, there might be several platters on a common spindle with a read/write head on the top and bottom of each platter. Figure 7-1 shows a hard disk assembly with the cover removed.

7-1 A hard disk system with the cover removed.

Why you need a hard drive

Hard drives are similar to floppy drives in many respects. Like floppies, they must be formatted and they have tracks, cylinders, and sectors. But they are much faster and can store much more data.

You might feel that you don't need a hard disk system. You would only feel this way if you have never used one. It is possible to operate a computer, even a 486, with just a single floppy drive, but you will be severely limited in what you can do and you will waste an enormous amount of time. I can't imagine anyone running a computer without a hard disk.

One reason for having a hard disk is for the convenience of storing programs. Most people who have been in the computer business for any length of time soon accumulate hundreds of programs on floppy disks. Unless you are better organized than I am, it is almost impossible to find what you want when you want it. If the floppies are copied to a hard disk, you can call them up within milliseconds anytime you need them.

Most of the software programs today, such as databases, spreadsheets, word processors, accounting programs, and others, might come to you on 20 diskettes or more. When these programs are used they sometimes need bits of data from each of the diskettes. You can see how difficult it would be to try to run programs such as these on a floppy system. If the program could run at all, it would have to frequently stop and wait for you to change diskettes. If the whole program is loaded on a hard disk, the data is available almost instantaneously.

Winchester origin

One of the first hard disk drive systems was developed by IBM. The system had a large 30Mb hard disk that could be removed and a 30Mb fixed internal hard disk.

The Winchester House, a tourist attraction, is located in San Jose, not far from an IBM plant. This house was built by the widow of the inventor of the Winchester .30–.30 rifle. Because the IBM hard disk was a 30/30 system, someone hung the name Winchester on it. The name stuck and all hard disks that use that original technology are known as Winchesters.

Choosing a hard disk

There are several factors to consider before deciding to buy a hard disk, including what you will use your computer for and how much you want to spend. I will briefly review some of the factors that should influence your decision.

Capacity

Buy the biggest you can afford. No matter how big it is, it will soon be filled up. Don't even think of buying anything less than 80Mb; better yet would be 200Mb. New software programs have become more and more user friendly and offer more and more options requiring more and more disk space.

Speed or access time

This is the time it takes a hard disk to locate and retrieve a sector of data. This includes the time it takes to move the head to the track, seat it, and read the data. For a high-end, very fast disk, this might be as little as 9 ms. Some of the older drives and systems required as long as 100 ms. An 85-ms hard drive might be okay for a slow XT. You can get by with a 28-ms drive on a 286 or a 386SX, but you will be much happier with a 15-ms to 19-ms system. Of course, the faster the hard disk, the more expensive it will be, so it depends on what you want your computer to do and how much you want to spend.

Type of drive—stepper or voice coil

Most of the less expensive hard drives use a stepper motor. It moves the heads in discrete steps or increments across the disk until they are over the track to be read or written. You can usually hear the heads as they move from track to track.

The voice coil type of hard drives are quieter, a bit faster, and more reliable, and, of course, more expensive. There might not be any marking on the drive to indicate whether it is a voice coil. The spec sheets for a voice coil drive will show that it has an odd number of heads. Actually, it has an even number of heads, one on the top and bottom of each platter, but one head and platter surface is used as a servo control for the other heads. The servo head follows a tracking system recorded by the factory. When a program calls for data to be read from a specific track, the servo head moves to that track very quickly and accurately. Because all of the heads move as one, the head that is supposed to read the data is also moved to the proper track.

A voice coil system is very quiet. Unless there is an LED (light-emitting diode) indicator on the front panel, you might not realize that it is operating. Most of the ESDI (enhanced small device interface) and high-end SCSI (small computer system interface) drives use voice coil technology.

Types of drives
Modified frequency modulation

Modified frequency modulation (MFM) was an early method developed for hard disk systems. In the early 1980s, Seagate Technology developed the ST506/412 interface for MFM, and it became the standard. This method formats several concentric tracks on a disk like those laid down on a floppy diskette. The MFM system divides the tracks into 17 sectors per track, with 512 bytes in each sector, so the MFM system does not lend itself to high-capacity drives. Most MFM systems are 20Mb to 100Mb. The transfer rate is 5Mb per second, with an access speed of 28 ms to 85 ms.

Most MFM systems use a stepper motor to move the heads from track to track. The MFM system is almost obsolete today, because it is slow and limited in capacity. On the plus side, MFM systems are quite reliable. If you can afford to wait a few milliseconds now and then, they are the least expensive drives you can buy.

Run length limited

The run length limited (RLL) system is a modification of the MFM system. The RLL drives, when used with an RLL controller, format 26 sectors per track, which allows 50 percent more data than on an MFM drive. For instance, a 20Mb drive can store 30Mb, a 40Mb can store 60Mb. They have a transfer rate of 7.5Mb per second, which is 50 percent faster than with MFM. The head access speed is about the same as that of MFM systems. Most of them also use the stepper motor head system. They are relatively inexpensive. Not all drives are capable of running RLL. Seagate uses an R after the model number to denote RLL drives.

Enhanced small device interface

The enhanced small device interface (ESDI, pronounced *ezdy)* is another modification of the MFM system. Most ESDI drives are large capacity, usually over 100Mb. ESDI drives can be formatted from 34 to 54 sectors per track, so they can store much more data than the 17 sectors of a standard MFM system. They have a very fast access speed, usually 15 ms to 18 ms, and a data transfer rate of 10Mb to 15Mb or more per second. They are ideal for high-end, disk-intensive computing, but they are fairly expensive.

Small computer system interface

Most drive manufacturers don't manufacture controllers. In many cases, you buy a drive from one manufacturer and buy a controller from another manufacturer. The small computer system interface (SCSI, pronounced *scuzzy*) drives have most of the disk controlling functions integrated into them. This makes sense because the control electronics can be optimally matched to the drive. They still require an interface card to transmit the data in 8-bit parallel, much like a parallel printer port. Because it can handle eight bits of data at once, it can have very fast transfer rates. The MFM, RLL, and ESDI drives are serial systems that transfer data one bit at a time over the lines. SCSI systems allow the recording of 26 to 54 sectors per track. They might also be more than twice as fast as MFM systems.

Integrated drive electronics

Several companies have developed drives with integrated drive electronics (IDE). The drives are similar to SCSI drives in that most of the control electronics are built into the drive. They were originally developed as a low-cost, low-end alternative to ESDI systems. When first developed they didn't have the speed or capacity of ESDI drives. But the technology has advanced and some of them are now equivalent to ESDI drives in capacity and speed. Many vendors have motherboards with a built-in interface and connector for the IDE. A single cable can be used to control two IDE drives. This saves the cost of a controller and also saves one of your slots. For other motherboards, a simple interface is needed to transfer data back and forth to the disk.

The IDE systems are very economical. Some of the low-cost ones might have access speeds of only 20 ms to 40 ms and use a head stepper motor. Several companies have models that use a voice coil system and provide high capacity, speed, and quality. The IDE drives have become the most common and most popular type of hard drive.

Cost per megabyte

Cost is always a factor to consider. If you figure the cost per megabyte, some of the low-end drives are actually more expensive than the high-end, large-capacity drives. To determine the cost per megabyte, divide the dollar amount by the number of megabytes. For instance, a Seagate ST251, a 42Mb MFM drive with a speed of 40 ms, is advertised for $229, plus $45 for a controller, for a total of $274. The per megabyte cost is $274/42Mb = $6.52. A Seagate ST3120A, a 106Mb IDE drive with a speed of 18 ms, is advertised in the same magazine for $359, plus $20 for an interface. The cost per megabyte for this drive is $379/106Mb = $3.57. This drive is more than twice as fast as the MFM drives and the cost per megabyte is about half that of the slower MFM drives. The cost of a drive will vary depending on the speed, capacity, manufacturer, and where and from whom you buy it.

Controllers

Hard disks need a controller card that plugs into one of the slots in the computer, or some type of interface, such as those for SCSI and IDE systems. In the past, very few of the hard disk companies made controllers for their disks, but today, there are several controller companies, many of which are now making them for their high-end EDSI and SCSI drives. The controllers and drives are then tested and sold as a pair.

There are many types of hard disk controllers (HDC) available. Some were developed specifically for 8-bit systems and others for the 16-bit AT-type systems, which include the 286, 386, and 486. An 8-bit controller can also be used on a 16-bit system, but a 16-bit card cannot be used on an 8-bit system. Most of the companies who make 16-bit controllers have integrated floppy disk controllers (FDC) into the same board. This saves space and is very convenient. These FDC/HDC boards can control 360K, 1.2Mb, 720K, and 1.44Mb disk drives, as well as two hard disks.

Note that the advertised price of disk drives might not include the controller or the necessary cables. An 8-bit card that controls hard drives only might cost as little as $40. A 16-bit card that controls both floppies and hard disks (FDC/HDC) might cost $45 to $150. Many companies advertise their drives bare or as a kit that contains the necessary cables and controllers.

Physical size

At one time floppy and hard drives were full height, or 3½ inches high and 5¼ inches wide. Today, only a few very high capacity drives are full height. The most common size today is half height, which is 1¾ inches high and 5¼ inches wide. The smaller size generally uses less power, has less mass, and is faster. Many companies are now making 3½-inch drives with up to 200Mb or more. Several companies are now making 2½-inch drives with 100Mb.

Hard cards

Several companies manufacture disks on plug-in cards. These cards have the disk on one end of the card and the controller on the other, making it very easy to add a second hard disk to your system. You simply remove the cover of your computer and plug the card in. There are no cables to worry about.

The original hard cards were 20Mb, but soon there were 30Mb, then 40Mb, and now many companies are manufacturing units with 100Mb or more. They are small and many of them have access speeds of 16 ms or less.

Removable media

Iomega has a high-capacity Bernoulli floppy diskette system. Their system allows the recording of up to 90Mb on a special floppy disk. A Bernoulli disk spins much faster than a standard floppy, forcing the flexible diskette to bend around the heads without actually touching them. This is in accordance with the principle discovered by the Swiss scientist, Jakob Bernoulli (1654–1705). The average seek time for a Bernoulli system is 32 ms, which is faster than some hard drives.

Bernoulli systems are ideal for areas where the data might be confidential. Each person in an office can have their own 90Mb floppy that can be removed and locked up. This system is also great for backing up a hard disk system. They might also be economical in another way. In a large company, there might be several computers. Separate copies of software would have to be purchased and installed on each machine. There might be 10 or more identical copies of software installed on each machine. Often, each person could be running a different software program, so most of the programs installed on those hard disks are sitting idle. If a single software program is installed on a removable disk, then it can be used as needed by any of the several users.

Iomega has had the field to themselves for several years, so the Bernoulli box has been a bit expensive at about $700 for a drive and about $100 for each diskette. But Brier Technology, Insite, and several other companies are now giving them some competition with new very high density systems. Prices should soon be quite reasonable for very high density systems.

Portable hard drives

Many people have portable and laptop computers without a hard disk. I am one of them. It was a big mistake. It is difficult to do any productive computing without a hard disk. You can't even load a simple word processor with spell check and thesaurus unless you have extra RAM. You can add RAM to the unit, but 2Mb of RAM cost almost as much as the entire laptop. The extra 2Mb works just like a fast hard drive. Unlike the RAM in your desktop, the extra RAM in a laptop retains its memory when the power is turned off as long as the battery holds its charge.

Most laptops don't have slots for a controller so all of the controller electronics are built into the disk. Pacific Rim and several other companies have developed a very small 2½-inch 20Mb hard disk that plugs into the parallel port. These systems can also be used with a desktop PC by plugging them into the parallel port. They can serve as a second hard disk or as a backup system. They can also be used to store classified data because they can be removed and locked up. If you are going to buy a laptop, I recommend that you buy one with a built-in hard disk.

Mean time before failure (MTBF)

If used long enough, every hard disk drive will eventually fail. Some manufacturers claim very high MTBF figures for their drives, as high as 40,000 to 150,000 hours. I have a few doubts as to the truth of these claims. If a drive is turned on for 8 hours a day, it would take almost 14 years to put 40,000 hours on it. It would take more than 51 years to put 150,000 hours on a drive at 8 hours a day.

Adding a second hard drive

A second hard drive can be very handy and beneficial even if you have lots of capacity on your first hard drive. There is always the possibility that your drive might fail, or the data on it might be lost. If your data is important, then it should be backed up.

Your second hard drive can be smaller than the first one and used just for backup. A hard drive can be backed up to another hard drive in just a few seconds. The probability that both drives will fail at the same time is quite small. For some operations where the data is extremely critical, you might want a second hard disk that mirrors the first one. The same data is written on both disks at the same time.

Formatting a hard disk

A floppy diskette is formatted in a single procedure, but a hard disk requires two levels of formatting a low level and a high level. The low level is critical to the performance of the drive, especially in setting the optimum interleave factor. To be done properly, low-level formatting requires sophisticated tools and some expertise. Because of this, the low-level format is performed on most hard disks before they are sold. This is especially true for SCSI and IDE drives.

You should receive some sort of documentation with your hard disk and controller. Almost all drives sold today have already been low-level formatted at the factory. Boot up from your floppy disk drive with the version of DOS that you intend to use. Make sure the diskette has the FDISK command on it. If it has been low-level formatted, type FDISK and it will allow you to partition the disk. If it accepts FDISK, just follow the directions on the screen. If you have more than one hard disk or have divided your disk into more than one partition, you will have to repeat the operation to high-level format each one.

CMOS ROM setup

The system ROM must be set up to recognize the type of hard disk that you have installed. The system must know how many heads, how many cylinders, the capacity, the landing zone for the heads, and several other things. Various model drives and drives from different manufacturers might all be different in some respect. The original IBM system grouped and recognized 15 different types in 1984. Most of today's systems recognize 46 different types. Many list a 47th type where it allows you to type in the various characteristics if your drive does not fit any of the listed types.

Compression

One way to add more space to your disk is to use compression. Compression has been around for several years. Most bulletin boards use one form or another of compression so they can save on data storage costs and on telephone and modem costs. It is possible to compress a file by half or more.

Most larger software companies ship their products in a compressed form. Many of them use the PK Zip format. They are unzipped, or expanded, when you load them on your hard disk.

In the past, one of the problems with compression was that it took a lot of time to compress and then expand. Today, several companies offer both software and hardware compression systems that are almost as fast as the fastest hard disk. One that I have been using, Stacker from Stac Electronics, can almost double the amount of space on any hard disk. They have both a software and a plug-in board version, or a software-only version. The software-only version lists for $99. If you have a 100Mb hard disk, it can double it. You cannot buy a hard disk for that amount. Using the board version makes it just a bit faster. The board version lists for $199.

I set up the software version on a 30Mb disk. When I do a CHKDSK, it tells me I have a 60Mb of usable space. When installed on the 20Mb Pacific Rim for my laptop, I get 40Mb. I have found it to be both fast and reliable. Figure 7-2 shows the Stacker board and software.

7-2 The Stacker compression software and hardware.

CD-ROM

The compact disk read-only memory (CD-ROM) industry is one of the fastest growing of all the computer peripherals. Sony, Hitachi, Phillips, JVC, Amdek, Panasonic, and several other companies are manufacturing these drives. These drives are all compatible and can be interfaced to a 386 with a plug-in board.

Since the time when the first man picked up a charred stick from his fire and drew a picture on a cave wall, man has been searching for newer and better ways to record data. There have been several noteworthy achievements—chiseled stone, writing on clay, papyrus, and Gutenberg with his press and the first printed Bible.

Today, we have mountains of printed matter. We also have a vast amount of data on magnetic disks and optical systems. We are almost inundated in a sea of information. Each day the haystacks become larger and it increasingly becomes more and more difficult to find the needle. The emerging CD-ROM technology makes it a lot easier to sift through the mountains of information to find what we are looking for.

These mountains of information are going to become even larger. There are thousands of CD-ROM disks available today. The off-the-shelf disks available cover a wide variety of subjects such as library and bookstore reference materials, general reference, literature, and art. There are disks on business, biology, medicine, physics, and most other branches of science and technology. There are disks on law, finances, geology, geography, government , and many other subjects. In time, there will be disks on almost any subject that is found in a large library.

Chapter 8

Backup

When you buy a software program, the first thing you should do is write-protect the diskettes. It is very easy to become distracted and write on a program diskette in error. This will probably ruin the program. The vendor might give you a new copy, but it will probably entail weeks of waiting and much paperwork.

Write-protect your software

If you are using 5¼-inch floppies, you should cover the square write-protect notch with a piece of opaque tape. Don't use Scotch™ or clear tape. The drive focuses a light through the square notch. If the light detector senses the light, it allows the diskette to be written on, read, or erased. If the notch is covered with opaque tape, the diskette can be read but not written on or erased. Some vendors now distribute their programs on diskettes without the square notch.

If you are using 3½-inch diskettes, you should move the small slide on the left rear of the case so that the square hole is open. The 3½-inch write-protect system is just the opposite of the 5¼-inch system. The 3½-inch system uses a microswitch. If the square hole is open, the switch allows the diskette to be read, but not written on or erased. If the slide is moved to cover the square hole, the diskette can be written on, read, or erased.

It takes less than a minute to write-protect a diskette, and it might save you weeks of valuable time. If a program diskette is ruined because it was not protected it might take weeks to get a replacement for the original. You might even have to buy a new program.

After you have made sure that the diskettes are write-protected, the second thing you should do is to use the DOS DISKCOPY command to make exact copies of your original diskettes. The originals should then be stored. Only the copies should be used. If you damage one, you can always make another copy from the original.

Protection from dirt and dust

There is a simple, easy way to protect your original program disks from dirt and dust. Seal them in a plastic sandwich bag.

Unerase software

Anyone who works with computers for any length of time is bound to make a few errors. One of the best protections against errors is to have a backup. The second best protection is to have a good utility program such as Norton Utilities or PC Tools. These programs can unerase a file or even unformat a disk. When a file is erased, DOS goes back to the FAT and deletes the first letter of each file name. All of the data remains on the disk unless a new file is written over it. If you have erased a file in error, or formatted a disk in error, do not do anything to it until you have tried using a recover utility. Don't use the DOS recover utility except as a last resort. Use Norton Utilities, Mace Utilities, PC Tools, DOSUTILS, or any of several other recovery utilities. These utilities allow you to restore the files by replacing the missing first letter of the file name.

Early versions of DOS made it very easy to incorrectly format your hard disk. If you happened to be on your hard disk and typed FORMAT, it would immediately begin to format your hard disk and wipe out everything. Later versions do not format unless you specify a drive letter. These versions also allow you to include a volume label, or name, on the drive when you format it by including the /v. Or you can add a label name later by using the command LABEL. If the drive has a volume label, it cannot be formatted unless the drive letter and correct volume name are specified. (You can display, delete, assign, or change the name of a volume by typing the command LABEL. The label name is also displayed when CHKDSK is run.)

Many people have erased files in error. They are only human so they will do it again. Some of them will not have backups or unerase software. In a fraction of a second, some of them will wipe out data that might be worth thousands of dollars. It might have taken hundreds of hours to accumulate and it might be impossible to duplicate. Yet many of these people have not backed up their precious data. Most of these people are fortunate enough not to have had a major catastrophe. Just as sure as there are earthquakes in California, if you use a computer long enough, you can look forward to at least one unfortunate disaster. There are thousands of ways to make mistakes and there is no sure way to prevent them. But if your data is backed up, it doesn't have to be a disaster. It is a lot better to be backed up than sorry.

Jumbled FAT

I talked about the all-important file allocation table (FAT) in the previous chapter. It keeps a record of the location of all the files on the disk. Parts of a file might be located in several sectors, but the FAT knows exactly where they are. If, for some reason, track 0, where the FAT is located, is damaged, erased, or becomes defective, then you will not be able to read or write to any of the files on the disk.

Because the FAT is so important, programs such as PC Tools and Mace Utilities make a copy of the FAT and store it in another location on the disk. Every time you add a file or edit one, the FAT changes, so these programs make a new copy every time the FAT is altered. If the original FAT is damaged, you can still get your data by using the backup FAT.

If you have a large-capacity hard disk and it fails, you might not be able to access or recover any of the data. But if a large disk is divided into several smaller drives, if one fails, you might still be able to recover the data on one of the other drives.

Head crash

The heads of a hard disk "fly" over the disk just a few microinches from the surface. They have to be close in order to detect the small magnetic changes in the tracks. The disk spins at 3600 rpms. If the heads contact the surface of the fast spinning disk, they can scratch it and ruin the disk.

A sudden jar or bump to the computer while the hard disk is spinning can cause the heads to crash. Of course, a mechanical failure or some other factor can also cause a crash. You should never move or bump your computer while the hard disk is running.

Most newer disks have a built-in park utility. When the power is removed, the head is automatically moved to the center of the disk where there are no tracks. But many of the older disks do not have this utility and it is possible for the head to crash if the power is suddenly removed, as in a power failure.

The technology of hard disk systems has improved tremendously over the last couple of years. But they are still mechanical devices, and as such, you can be sure that eventually they will wear out, fail, or crash.

Most hard disks are now relatively bug free. Manufacturers quote mean time before failure (MTBF) figures of several thousand hours. But these figures are only an average. There is no guarantee that a disk won't fail sooner than its MTBF. A hard disk is made up of several mechanical parts. If it is used long enough, it will wear out or fail. Many vendors list MTBF figures of 40,000 to 150,000 hours, which means that the disk should last for several years. But there are lots of businesses that do nothing but repair hard disks that have crashed or failed.

A failure can be frustrating and time-consuming and can make you feel utterly helpless. In the unhappy event of a crash, it is possible that some of your data might be recovered, depending on the severity of the crash.

Crash recovery

There are companies that specialize in recovering data and rebuilding hard disks. Many of them have sophisticated tools and software that can recover some data if the disk is not completely ruined. If it is possible to recover any of the data, Ontrack Computer Systems, among others, can probably do it. Look in the computer magazine ads. A couple of companies that I have used to recover data are California Disk Drive Repair and Rotating Memory Service. They supplied the crashed disk for the photo in Fig. 8-1. They were unable to recover any data from the disk. It was much more severe than most crashes.

8-1 A hard disk that has crashed.

The cost for recovery services can be rather expensive, but if you have data that is critical, it is well worth it. However, it is a whole lot cheaper to have a backup.

Small logical drives are better

Early versions of DOS would not recognize a hard disk larger than 32Mb. DOS now allows you to have a drive C or D of 512Mb or more. Don't do it. If this large hard disk crashes, you might not be able to recover any of the data. If the same disk is divided into several smaller logical drives and one of the logical sections fails, it might be possible to recover data in the unaffected logical drives.

Some reasons why people don't and why they should back up
Don't have the time

This is not a good excuse. If your data is worth anything at all, it is worth backing up. It takes only a few minutes to back up a large hard disk with some of the newer software.

Too much trouble

It is a bit of trouble unless you have an expensive automated tape backup system. Backup can require a bit of disk swapping, labeling, and storing, but with a little organizing, it can be done. If you keep all of the disks together, you don't have to label each one. Just stack them in order, put a rubber band around them, and put a label on the first one.

Yes, it is a bit of trouble to make backups. But if you don't have a backup, consider the time it will take to redo the files from a disk that has crashed. The time and trouble of making a backup are infinitesimal.

Don't have the necessary disks, software, or tools

Depending on the amount of data to be backed up and the software used, it might require 50 to 100 disks. Of course, it will require a lot fewer if high-density disks are used. Again, it takes only a few minutes and a few disks to make a backup of only the data that has been changed or altered. In most cases, the same disks can be reused the next day to update the files. There are several discount mail-order houses that sell 360K disks for as little as 25 cents apiece, 39 cents each for 1.2Mb and 720K, and 59 cents each for 1.44Mb. Several discount companies are listed in chapter 6.

Failures and disasters only happen to other people

People who believe this are those who have never experienced a disaster. There is nothing you can say to convince them. They just have to learn the hard way.

A few other reasons
why you should back up

General failure

Outside of ordinary care, there is little you can do to prevent a general failure. It could be a component in the hard disk electronics or in the controller system, or any one of a thousand other things. Even a power failure during a read/write operation can cause data corruption.

Theft and burglary

Computers are easy to sell so they are a favorite target for burglars. It is bad enough to lose a computer, but many computers have hard disks filled with data that is even more valuable than the computer.

Speaking of theft, it might be a good idea to put your name and address on several of the files on your hard disk. It is also a good idea to scratch identifying marks on the back and bottom of the case. You should also write down the serial numbers of your monitor and drives.

Another good idea is to store your backup files in an area away from your computer. This way, there is less chance of losing both your computer and your backups in a burglary or fire.

Archival

Another reason to back up is for archival purposes. No matter how large the hard disk is, it will eventually fill up with data. Quite often, there are files that are no longer used or they might only be used once in a great while. I keep copies of all the letters that I write on disk. I have hundreds of them. Rather than erase the old files or old letters, I put them on a disk and store them away.

Fragmentation

After a hard disk has been used for a while, files begin to be fragmented. The data is recorded on concentric tracks in separate sectors. If part of a file is erased or changed, some of the data might be placed in a sector on track 20 and another part on track 40. There might be open sectors on several tracks because portions of data have been erased. Hunting all over the disk can slow the disk down. If the disk is backed up completely, then erased, the files can be restored so that they are recorded in contiguous sectors. The utility programs mentioned earlier can unfragment a hard disk by copying portions of the disk to memory and rearranging the data in contiguous files.

Data transfer

Often, it is necessary to transfer a large amount of data from one hard disk to another. This can be accomplished quite easily and quickly using a good backup program. It is easy to make several copies that can be distributed to others in the company. This method can be used to distribute data, company policies and procedures, sales figures, and other information to several people in a large office or company. The data can also be shipped or mailed to branch offices, customers, or to others almost anywhere.

Methods of backup
Software
There are two main types of backup: image and file oriented. An *image backup* is an exact bit-for-bit copy of the hard disk, copied as a continuous stream of data. This type of backup is rather inflexible and does not allow for a separate file backup or restoration. The *file oriented* backup identifies and indexes each file separately. With this type of backup, separate files or directories can be backed up and restored. It can be very time-consuming to have to backup an entire 40Mb or more each day. With a file oriented system, once a full backup is made, it is necessary to make only incremental backups of those files that have been changed or altered.

DOS stores an archive attribute in each file directory entry. When a file is created, DOS turns the archive attribute flag on. If the flag is backed up using the DOS BACKUP command or any of the commercial backup programs, the archive attribute flag is turned off. If this file is later altered or changed, DOS will turn the attribute back on. At the next backup, you can have the program search the files and look for the attribute flag. You can then back up only those files that have been altered or changed since the last backup. You can view or modify a file's archive attribute by using the DOS ATTRIB command.

There are several good software programs on the market that allow you to use a 5¼-inch or 3½-inch disk drive to back up your data. Again, you should have backups of all your master software, so don't worry about backing up your software every day. Because DOS stamps each file with the date and time it was created, it is easy to back up only those files that were created after a certain date and time.

Once the first backup is made, only data that has been changed or updated needs to be added to subsequent backups. Most backup programs can recognize whether a file has been changed since the last backup. Most of the them can also look at the data that is stamped on each file and back up only those within a specified date range.

BACKUP.COM   One of the least expensive methods of backup is using the MS-DOS commands BACKUP.COM and RESTORE.COM. These methods are time-consuming and rather difficult to use, however, they'll do the job if nothing else is available.

A few of the commercial backup programs available are discussed below. There are many others. Check the computer magazines for ads and reviews.

Norton Backup   Norton Backup is one of the newest and fastest backup programs on the market. It is also one of the easiest to use. It compresses the data so that fewer disks are needed.

Norton Desktop for Windows   Norton and Symantec have now merged. This software package has several very useful utilities, including emergency unerase, manual or automatic backup, utilities for creating batch files, and management of directories and files under Windows.

Fastback   Fastback Plus was one of the first backup software programs that was fast. It is easy to learn and use, and compresses the data so that fewer floppy disks are needed.

Back-It 4   Back-It 4, from Gazelle Systems, uses very high-density data compression, as much as 3 to 1. It is also very fast and uses a sophisticated error correction routine. Unlike some of the other systems, Back-It 4 allows you to use different format floppies at the same time.

PC Tools   PC Tools comes bundled with a very good backup program. The backup program is now being sold separately to anyone who doesn't want to buy the whole bundle.

XTree   XTree is an excellent shell program for disk and file management. It has several functions that make computing much easier. You can use it to copy files from one directory or disk to another. I often use it to make backups when I only have a few files to back up.

Q-DOS III   Q-DOS III, from Gazelle Systems, is another excellent shell program that is similar to XTree. It can be used to select and copy files to another hard disk or to floppies.

DOS XCOPY   The XCOPY command is part of MS-DOS versions higher than 3.2. There are several switches that can be used with XCOPY. (A switch is a /.) For instance, XCOPY C:*.* A:/A copies only those files that have their archive attribute set to on. It does not reset the attribute flag. XCOPY C:*.* A:/M copies the files, then resets the flag. Whenever a disk on A: is full, you merely have to insert a new floppy and hit F3 to repeat the last command. This continues copying all files that have not been backed up. XCOPY C:*.* A:/D:03-15-92 copies only those files created after 15 March 1992. There are several other very useful switches that can be used with XCOPY.

Tape

Several different tape backup systems are on the market. Tape backup is easy, but it can be relatively expensive—$400 to over $1000 for a drive unit, and $5 to $20 for a tape cartridge. Most of them require the use of a controller that is similar to a disk controller, so they will use one of your precious slots. Unless they are used externally, they also require the use of one of the disk mounting areas.

One of the big problems with software backup is that you have to sit there and put in a new disk when one is full. One big plus for tape is that it can be set up so that it is done automatically. You don't have to worry about forgetting to back up or about wasting your time doing it.

Digital audio tape

Several companies are offering digital audio tape (DAT) systems for backing up large hard disk systems. DAT systems offer storage capacities as high as 1.3Gb on a very small cartridge. DAT systems use a helical scan-type recording that is similar to that used for video recording. Digital audio tapes are 4 millimeters wide (0.156 inches).

Very high-density disk drives

Several companies are now making extended density 2.8Mb floppies and very high-density 20Mb floppy disk drives. Insite, Brier Technology, and several other companies have developed 3½-inch floppy disks that can store 20Mb. The Bernoulli drive can put 44Mb on a 5¼-inch floppy disk.

Even though they cost a bit more, a high-density floppy drive can be more advantageous than tape. A high-density floppy has much more utility, possibly even obviating the need for a hard disk. For more details on these drives refer to chapter 6.

Second hard disk

The easiest and fastest of all methods of backup is to have a second hard disk. It is very easy to install a second hard disk because most controllers have the capability of controlling a second hard disk. You just have to make sure that the second hard disk will work with your first disk. With a second hard disk as a backup, you will not need a backup software package. A good backup software package can cost $200 or more. You can probably buy a second hard disk for this amount.

An average hard disk has an access speed of about 40 ms. Floppy disks operate at about 300 ms, which can seem like an eternity compared to the speed of even the slowest hard disk. Depending on the number of files, how fragmented the data is on the disk, and the access speed, a second hard disk can back up 20Mb in a matter of seconds. To back up 20Mb using even the fastest software requires 15 to 20 minutes. It also requires that you do a lot of disk swapping. Depending on the type of disks you use for backup and the type of software, it might require 50 to 60 of the 360K disks, 17 of the 1.2Mb disks, or 14 of the 1.44Mb disks. Some of the latest backup software makes extensive use of data compression, so fewer disks are needed.

Another problem with using software backup is that it is often difficult to find a particular file. Most backup software stores the data in a system that is not the same as DOS files. Usually there is no directory like that provided by DOS. Even the DOS BACKUP files show only a control number when you check the directory.

External plug-in hard drives

Several companies are now manufacturing small 20Mb to 80Mb hard disks that operate off the parallel or serial connector. Many of them are battery powered so they can be used with laptops. They can also be used to back up data from a large desktop system or to transfer data from one system to another. Pacific Rim Systems makes an excellent 20Mb system. By installing the Stacker compression software on this 20Mb hard disk, it can store about 40Mb.

Hard cards

You can buy a hard disk on a card for $300 to $600 depending on the capacity and the company. The higher-capacity disks are usually rather expensive. Compression software can also be used on these disks. It might be worthwhile to install a card in an empty slot and dedicate it to backup.

If there are no empty slots, you might even consider plugging in the card once a week to make a backup and removing the card until it is needed again. This entails removing the cover from the machine each time. But I remove the cover to my computer so often that I only use one screw on it to provide grounding. I can remove and replace my cover in a very short time.

Failure and frustration

Rotating Memory Service supplied the disk for the photo in Fig. 8-2. The hard disk failed and the person became so frustrated that he took out a .357 Magnum and shot it three times. I know exactly how that person must have felt. I have often felt the same way. But lucky for my computer, I don't own a gun.

No matter what type of system or method is used, if your data is worth anything at all, you should be using something to back it up. You might be one of the lucky ones and never need it. But it is much better to be backed up than to be sorry.

8-2 A hard disk that was shot three times with a .357 Magnum.

Chapter 9

Input devices

Before a computer can do anything, it must have data. Data can be input from a disk, modem, mouse, scanner, bar-code reader, voice, fax, or on-line from a mainframe or a network. But by far the most common way to put data into a computer is by way of the keyboard. For most common applications, it is impossible to operate a computer without a keyboard.

Keyboards

The keyboard is your personal connection with your computer. If you do much typing, it is very important that you get a keyboard that suits you. Not all keyboards are the same. Some have a light mushy touch; some heavy. Some have noisy keys, others are silent with little feedback.

A need for standards

Typewriter keyboards are fairly standard. There are only 26 letters in the alphabet and a few symbols, so most QWERTY typewriters have about 50 keys. But I have had several computers over the last few years and every one of them has had a different keyboard. The main typewriter characters aren't changed or moved very often, but some of the very important control keys like Esc, Ctrl, Prt Scr,\ , the function keys, and several others are moved all over the keyboard. IBM can be blamed for most of the changes.

The original IBM keyboard had the very important and often-used Esc key just to the left of the 1 key in the numeric row. The 84-key keyboard moved the Esc key over to the top row of the keypad. The tilde (~) and grave (`) key was moved to the original Esc position (to the left side of the 1). The IBM 101-key keyboard moved the Esc key back to its original position.

For some unknown reason IBM also decided to move the function keys to the top of the keyboard above the numeric keys. This is quite frustrating for WordStar users because the Ctrl key and the function keys are used quite often. The original position made them very easy to access.

There are more than 400 different keyboards available in the United States. Many people make their living by typing on a keyboard. Many large companies have systems that count the number of keystrokes that an employee makes during a shift. If the employee fails to make a certain number of keystrokes, then that person can be fired. Can you imagine the problems when the person has to frequently learn a new keyboard? There definitely should be some sort of standards. Figure 9-1 shows three keyboards; each one of them has a different key arrangement.

Model switch

The PC, XT, AT, 80286, 80386, and 80486 keyboards all have the same connectors. Any keyboard will plug into any of these machines, but the PC and XT keyboards have different electronics and scan frequencies. An older PC or XT keyboard can be plugged into an 80286 or 80386 machine, but it will not operate.

9-1 Three keyboards, each one with different key positions.

Most keyboards now have a switch on the back that allows them to be switched so that they can be used on a PC, XT, or AT-type 286, 386, or 486 machines. Some of the newer keyboards can electronically sense the type of computer they are attached to and automatically switch to that type.

How a keyboard works

The keyboard is actually a computer in itself. It has a small microprocessor with its own ROM. The computerized electronics of the keyboard eliminate the bounce of the keys, can determine when you hold a key down for repeat, can store up to 20 or more keystrokes, and can determine which key was pressed first if you press two at a time. The newer microprocessors for the AT-type machines are more complex and sophisticated than the early PC types.

In addition to the standard BIOS chips on your motherboard, there is a special keyboard BIOS chip. Each time a key is pressed, a unique signal is sent to the BIOS. This signal is made up of binary 0s and 1s, or rather a voltage that is turned on and off a certain number of times within a time frame.

Each time a 5-volt line is turned on for a certain amount of time, it represents a 1, when it is off for a certain amount of time, it represents a 0. In ASCII code, if letter A is pressed, the binary code for 65 is generated—1 0 0 0 0 0 1.

Special keys

The main part of the keyboard is very similar to a typewriter layout. However, there are some extra keys that I will describe. It is possible to press two or more special keys at the same time for some functions. Pressing keys such as the Shift, Ctrl, Alt, and F (function) keys, in conjunction with other keys, gives a very large number of virtual keys.

Function keys   *Function* keys are multipurpose keys. What they do is usually dependent on the software you are using at the time. Many software programs use the function keys to accomplish a goal with a minimum of keystrokes. Often, the function of the keys is displayed somewhere on the screen.

On older keyboards the function keys were located to the left of the standard keys. The 101 systems place them above the top row of numerals. The older keyboards had 10 function keys, the 101 keyboards have 12.

Macros for the function keys are already set up in many software programs. For example, WordStar has an installation menu that allows you to program the function keys. There are 10 functions available using each function key alone, such as on-line help, underline, boldface, delete a line, delete a word, etc. There are 30 more functions available by using the function keys with the Ctrl, Shift, and Alt keys.

DOS and function keys   DOS provides a number of macros or shortcuts by using the function keys.

F1—redisplay each character   If you enter a DOS command, pressing F1 will redisplay the command each time the key is pressed.

F2—change part of last command   If you enter a DOS command and you want to change part of it, you can enter a letter of the command and all of the command up to that letter will be displayed. You can then change the command from that point onward. This can save a few keystrokes.

F3—redisplay last command   The F3 function key redisplays the entire command previously entered. For instance, you can enter the command COPY A: B:. When it has finished, if you want to make a second copy, just press F3 and the command will come up again. All you have to do is press Enter.

F4—use part of last command   If a command is entered and you want to reuse the last portion of if, just press a letter of the command and the portion from that letter to the end of the command will be displayed.

F6—end of file character   When you create a file, such as a .BAT file, DOS has to know when the file ends. F6 puts the ^Z to mark the end of your files.

Numbers   There are two sets of numbers on the keyboard. The row across the top is very similar to the keys on a standard typewriter. They also have the standard symbols that are available when the shift and a number key is pressed. The second set of numbers is arranged in a configuration similar to a calculator keypad. This makes it very easy to input large amounts of numeric data. The numbers on this set of keys are active only when the Num Lock is on. When the Num Lock is off, the special keys move the cursor about the keyboard.

Arrow keys   The down arrow on the 2 key moves the cursor down one line. The up arrow on the 8 key moves it up one line. The left arrow on the 4 moves the cursor to the left; the right arrow on the 6 moves it to the right. The 101-key keyboard added a second set of arrow keys between the main keys and the number pad.

Home and end keys   The Home on the 7 key moves the cursor to the upper left-hand corner of the screen. The End on the 1 key moves it to the bottom of the screen or the end of the text.

PgDn and PgUp (page down and page up)   PgDn on the 3 key causes the next page to be displayed on the screen. PgUp causes the computer to page backwards through the file.

Ins (insert)   Ins on the 0 key allows text to be inserted without writing over the present text. The text will continue to move to the right to allow text to be entered. Ins works like a toggle switch; it turns on or off each time it is pressed. With the Ins off, anything typed will replace any character at the cursor.

Del (delete)   The Del on the period or decimal key deletes the character at the cursor. All characters to the right will move to the left to fill in the gap.

The 101-key keyboards have additional and separate PgDn, PgUp, Ins, Home, End, and Del keys between the main keys and the numeric pad.

Esc (escape)   Most programs utilize this key in some way to leave a program, to erase a line, or for other functions.

Prt Scr (print screen)   By pressing the Prt Scr key, anything on the screen is sent to the printer and printed out.

* (asterisk)   The * key has different meanings depending on the program or mode you are in. For most calculating programs, it means times or multiplication. For instance, 4*15 means 4 times 15. In DOS, the * can be used as a wildcard for copying or manipulating files. For instance, if you have several files that have the extension .bak and you wanted to erase all of them, you can give the single command Del *.bak.

Scroll lock   The scroll lock has different functions in different programs. Some software programs use it to disable the cursor control keys.

Break   When the Ctrl key is pressed along with the Break key, the computer usually interrupts what it is doing. Pressing Ctrl-C does about the same thing. On some keyboards, Break is on the same key with Scroll Lock.

Backspace   The backspace key is a left-pointing arrow at the far right on the standard numeral key row. It moves the cursor backwards one character at a time. In most programs, it erases the character to the left of it as it moves backward.

Return or Enter   This key is used to tell the computer that you have finished that particular line or entry. In many word processors, the Return or Entry key is used only at the end of a paragraph. When the cursor reaches the end of the right margin, most word processors automatically wrap around and send the cursor to the left for the next line.

Shift   There are two Shift keys that operate the same as those on a typewriter. They are used to input uppercase letters and the standard symbols on the numeric keys.

Caps Lock   This key is similar to the *shift lock* key on a typewriter, except that it affects the letters of the alphabet only. If you want to type in a $ sign for instance, you must use the shift key whether or not the Caps Lock is on. When the Caps Lock is on you can also use the shift keys to type a lowercase letter of the alphabet.

Ctrl (control)   The Ctrl key is used in conjunction with several other keys for a variety of purposes. If you ask to view a long directory with the DIR command, it might scroll up the screen very quickly. You can use Ctrl-S to stop it, then press any key to start it again. Ctrl-C will abort the directory and return you to the prompt sign of whatever directory or file you were in.

Tab   The Tab key has a left-pointing and a right-pointing arrow with a bar at the end of each arrow tip. The bottom arrow that points to the right works just like the Tab key on a typewriter. The top arrow that points left moves the cursor backwards to tab stops when the Shift key is used with it. Not all programs use backward tabs.

Alt (alternate)   The Alt key can have a variety of functions depending on the particular software program. It is most often used with Ctrl and Del to reboot or reset the computer system. For instance, you might give the computer a command to perform a certain task. It will drop everything and try to do it. If part of the program is missing or for some reason the task cannot be performed, the computer might continue and ignore any pleas from you to come back. Often, there is no way out except to use Ctrl-Alt-Del to reset the system. This clears the memory and anything that has not been saved to disk is erased. There are times when even this warm boot will not clear the computer. In this case, you will have to turn the power off and back on to clear it.

Other special key functions   The backslash (\) is used by DOS to denote a subdirectory. To change from one subdirectory to another, you must type CD\ , then the directory name. If no name is given, you will be returned to the root directory. The backslash should not be confused with the slash. If you use the slash where the backslash should be used, you will get an error message, or if it is part of a program, the program will not work.

The slash (/) is also called the virgule, the shilling, and the solidus. In calculations it is used as the division symbol.

Other symbols include < for less than; > for greater than; the caret (^) for exponents; and +, –, and = for other math functions.

Reprogramming key functions

The keys can be changed by various software programs to represent almost anything you want them to. One thing that makes learning computers so difficult is that every software program uses the special keys in a different way. You might learn all the special keys that WordStar uses, but if you want to use a word processor such as WordPerfect or Microsoft Word, you have to learn the special commands and keys that they use.

Major word processors, spreadsheets, and other software programs will let you set up macro programs. A macro program lets you record a series of keystrokes, such as your name and address, the time and date, or any other frequently used item, repeat it by pressing just one or two keys.

Keyboard sources

Keyboard preference is strictly a matter of individual taste. Key Tronic makes some excellent keyboards. They are the IBM of the keyboard world. Their keyboards have set the standard. Key Tronic keyboards have been copied by the clone makers, even to the extent of using the same model numbers.

Key Tronic offers several models. They even let you change the little springs under the keys to different tensions. The standard is 2 ounces, but you can configure the key tension to whatever you like. You can install 1, 1.5, 2, 2.5, or 3-ounce springs for an extra $15. You can also exchange the positions of the Caps Lock and Ctrl keys. Key Tronic keyboards have several other functions that can be found in their large manual.

There are hundreds of good keyboards for $35 to $90. Look through any computer magazine. If at all possible, try the keyboard out and compare. If you are buying a system through the mail, ask about keyboard options.

Specialized keyboards

Several companies have developed specialized keyboards. I list only a few of them below.

Often, I need to do minor calculations. The computer is great for calculations. There are several programs, such as SideKick, Windows, and WordStar, with built-in calculators. A keyboard from the Shamrock Company and from Jameco has a built-in solar-powered calculator where the number pad is located, and the calculator can be used whether the computer is on or not.

Focus Electronics has a series of specialized keyboards with built-in calculators, function keys in both locations, extra asterisk and backslash keys, and several other goodies. Their FK-5001 keyboard has eight cursor arrow keys, allowing the cursor to move diagonally up or down from any of the four corners of the screen. The speed of the cursor movement can be varied by using the 12 function keys. These eight cursor keys will do just about everything that a mouse can do.

The Datacomp DFK 2010 keyboard is similar to the FK-5001. It has the function keys at the top and left side and allows you to switch the Ctrl key back to where it is supposed to be. It also has the diagonal arrow cursor keys like the FK-5001.

Besides their standard keyboards, Key Tronic has developed a large number of specialized keyboards. Instead of a keypad, one has a touch pad. This pad can operate in several different modes. One mode allows it to act as a cursor pad. By using your finger or a stylus, the cursor can be moved much the same as with a mouse. The touchpad keyboard comes with templates for several popular programs, such as WordStar, WordPerfect, DOS, and Lotus 1-2-3.

Another Key Tronic model has a bar-code reader attached to it. This can be extremely handy if you have a small business that uses bar codes. This keyboard is ideal for a computer in a point of sale system.

Keyboard covers

There are special plastic covers that can protect against spills, dust, or other environmental hazards. There are some areas, such as the floor of a manufacturing area, where a cover is absolutely essential. Most of the covers are made from soft plastic that is molded to fit over the keys. They are pliable, but they do slow down the serious typist.

Several companies manufacture custom covers. One company is CompuCover, another is Tech-Cessories. There are well over 400 different keyboards used in the United States. If you count the foreign keyboards, there are probably over 4000 different types worldwide. These companies claim that they can provide a cover for most of them. The average cover costs about $25. This is a bit expensive for just a bit of shrink-type plastic. One reason they are so expensive is that there are so many different keyboards. Quality Computer Products says that its QCP 101 keyboard is spill proof.

Mouse systems

One of the biggest reasons for the success of the Macintosh is that it is easy to use. With a mouse and icons, all you have to do is point and click. You don't have to learn a lot of commands and rules. A person who knows nothing about computers can become productive in a very short time. People in the DOS world finally took note of this and began developing programs and applications, such as Windows, for the IBM and compatibles.

There are dozens of companies now manufacturing mice. Many software programs were developed to be used without a mouse, but they operate much faster and better with a mouse. To be productive, a mouse is essential for programs such as Windows 3.0, CAD, paint and graphics, and others.

You can't just plug in a mouse and start using it. The software, whether Windows, WordStar, or a CAD program, must recognize and interface with the mouse. Mouse companies developed software drivers that allow their mouse to operate with various programs. The drivers are usually supplied on a diskette. The Microsoft Mouse is considered to be a standard, so most other companies emulate the Microsoft driver.

Types of mice

There is no standard type of mouse. Some companies use optics with an LED that shines on a reflective grid. As the mouse is moved across the grid, the reflected light is picked up by a detector and sent to the computer to move the cursor. If you demand very close tolerances, the spacings of the grid for an optical mouse might not provide sufficient resolution. You might be better off with a high-resolution mouse that utilizes a ball.

The ball-type mouse has a small rubber ball on the underside that contacts the desktop. As the mouse is moved, the ball turns. Inside the mouse, two flywheels contact the ball, one for horizontal and one for vertical movements. You don't need a grid for the ball-type mouse, but you do need about a square foot of clear desk space to move the mouse about. The ball picks up dirt so it should be cleaned often. Figure 9-2 shows a mouse with the ball removed for cleaning.

Some of the less-expensive mice have a resolution capability of only 100 to 200 dots per inch (DPI). Logitech has developed a HiREZ mouse that has a resolution of 320 DPI.

IMCS put their mouse in a pen-like configuration. Their Mouse Pen has a barrel about 6 inches long and about ½-inch square. The foot of the pen has a small ball that functions exactly like a mouse, and it can be moved just as if you are writing. It has two buttons on the barrel.

Number of buttons

The Macintosh mouse has only one button. That doesn't give you much choice except to point and click. Almost all of the PC mice have at least two buttons, which

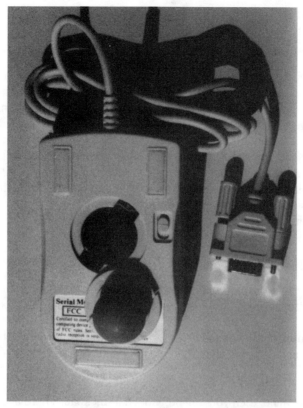

9-2 A mouse with the ball removed for cleaning.

gives the user three choices: (1) click the left button, (2) click the right button, or (3) click both buttons at the same time. Some mice have three control buttons. With three buttons the user has a possible seven choices. Despite all these choices, most software requires that only two of the buttons be used, one at a time.

Interfaces

Most mice require about 5 volts. Some come with a small plug-in transformer that should be plugged into your power strip. Some of them let you insert an adapter between the keyboard cable connector and the motherboard connector. Some mice require the use of one of your serial ports for their input to the computer. This might cause a problem if you already have devices such as a serial printer using COM1 and a modem on COM2. You might have to buy a board and use one of your plug-in slots to provide a serial interface for the COM ports. Some of the motherboards have ports built into the board.

Microsoft, Logitech, and several other mouse companies have developed a bus mouse. It interfaces directly with the bus and does not require the use of one of your COM ports. However, the system comes with a board that requires the use of one of your slots. Most mouse systems come with several software packages and drivers that allow the mouse to be used with several programs.

Cost

You can buy a fairly good mouse for $50 to $100. One factor in the cost is that some companies include options of software packages and other goodies with their products.

Another cost factor is the resolution. Some have a resolution of only 100 DPI; the better ones have a resolution of 200 DPI to 350 DPI. The higher resolution is necessary for some CAD, and critical design work that requires close tolerances.

Some mouse systems are advertised for as little as $30. These would probably be perfectly all right for point and click work with icons. Of course, higher-resolution systems are going to cost more. It is best to call the companies for their latest price lists and spec sheets. There are many companies that manufacture mouse systems. Check the ads in the computer magazines listed in chapter 15.

Trackballs

A trackball is a mouse turned upside down. Like the mouse, a trackball must have a voltage from a transformer or other source. It also requires a serial port or a slot if it is a bus type.

Instead of moving the mouse to move the ball, the ball is moved by your fingers. Trackballs are usually larger than the ball in a mouse, so they normally have higher resolution.

Trackballs do not require as much desk space as the ordinary mouse. If your desk is as cluttered as mine, then you definitely need a trackball. There are several companies that manufacture trackballs. Look through the computer magazines for ads.

Keyboard/trackball combinations

Amtac, Chicony, and several other companies have keyboards with a trackball built into the right side. This gives you the benefits and capabilities of a mouse without using up extra desk space. The trackball is compatible with the standard Microsoft and mouse systems.

I bought a Chicony keyboard with a trackball for $68. This is a real bargain when you consider that several other companies offer a stand-alone trackball that costs $75 or more. Several other companies make combination trackball/keyboard systems. Check computer magazines for ads.

Digitizers and graphics tablets

Graphics tablets and digitizer tablets are similar to a flat drawing pad or drafting table. Most of them use some type of pointing device that can translate movement into digitized output. Some tablets are rather small, and some are as large as a standard drafting table. They can cost as little as $150 to more than $1500. Most of them have a very high resolution, are very accurate, and are intended for precision drawing.

Some of the tablets have programmable overlays and function keys. Some work with a mouse-like device, a penlight, or a pencil-like stylus. The tablets can be used for circuit design, CAD programs, graphics, freehand drawing, and even for text and data input. The most common use is with CAD software.

Most tablets are serial devices, although some require their own interface board. Many of them are compatible with Microsoft and mouse systems. The Wiz is one low-cost combination digitizer and mouse from CalComp.

Scanners and optical character readers

Most large companies have mountains of memos, manuals, documents, and files that must be maintained, revised, and updated periodically. If a document is bound, the whole manual or document might have to be retyped and reissued. If a manual or document is in a loose leaf form, then only those pages that change need to be retyped.

Several companies manufacture optical character readers (OCRs) that can scan a line of printed type, recognize each character, and input that character into a computer just as if it were typed in from a keyboard. Once the data is in the computer, a word processor can be used to revise or change the data, and print it out again.

The printed data can also be entered into a computer and stored on floppies or a hard disk. If copies of the printed matter are stored in a computer they can be searched very quickly for any item. Many times I have spent hours going through printed manuals looking for certain items. If the data had been in a computer, I could have found the information in just minutes.

9-3 The Typist, a hand-held scanner, and its interface board.

Optical character readers have been around for several years. When they first came out, they cost $6000 to more than $15,000. OCRs were very limited in the character fonts they could recognize, and they were unable to handle graphics at all. Today, many full-page scanners are fairly inexpensive, starting at about $650. Some hand-held scanners, which are rather limited, might be as low as $200. Figure 9-3 shows a very good hand-held scanner from Caere. The more expensive models usually have the ability to recognize a large number of fonts and graphics.

Houston Instruments specializes in manufacturing plotters. They have developed a scanning head for one of their plotters that can scan a large drawing, digitize the lines and symbols, and input them to a computer. The drawing can then be changed and replotted very easily.

There are many manufacturers of input devices. Look in any of the computer magazines listed in chapter 15. You will see ads for all types of keyboards, scanners, mice, and other input devices. Some magazines, such as *PC Sources* and *Computer Shopper,* have a separate product list in the back. It is a great help. However, they list only those products that are advertised in their magazine that month.

Of course, there are many good products that can't afford the high cost of magazine ads. If you live in a large city, there are local computer stores. Also, computer swaps can be a very good source for equipment and information.

Chapter 10

Modems
and
faxes

Each day, millions of people risk their lives fighting traffic as they commute back and forth to work. Many of these people have jobs that could allow them to stay home, work on a computer, and send the data to the office via a modem or a facsimile. Even if the person had to buy their own computer, modem, and fax machine, it still might be worth it. You could save the cost of gasoline, auto maintenance, and lower insurance, not to mention your sanity. Being able to work at home is ideal for those who have young children, for the handicapped, or for anyone who hates traffic.

Modems

A modem is an electronic device that allows a computer to use an ordinary telephone line to communicate with other computers that are equipped with a modem. Modem is a contraction of the words *modulate* and *demodulate*.

Why the need for a modem

The voice signals sent over a telephone line are analog voltages. When you speak into the mouthpiece, a diaphragm moves back and forth due to the pressure of the sound waves. This diaphragm creates an analog alternating voltage that goes up and down to match the frequency and intensity of the sound waves. This voltage is sent out over the telephone lines. The earpiece on the other end of the telephone line is like a miniature loudspeaker. The small speaker in the earpiece responds to the received signals and vibrates to re-create a fairly reasonable copy of the sound that was input at the other end of the line.

Computer data is usually in digital form. It might be 5 volts of direct current that is turned on and off to create binary 0s and 1s. The modem modulates the digital data from a computer and turns it into analog alternating voltages for transmission. At the receiving end, a similar modem demodulates the analog voltage back into a digital form.

It is easy to use a telephone to communicate with any one of several million persons anywhere in the world. A computer, with telecommunications capabilities, can just as easily communicate with several million other computers in the world. They can access over 10,000 bulletin boards in the United States. They can take advantage of electronic mail, faxes, up-to-the-minute stock market quotations, and a large number of other on-line services, such as home shopping, travel agencies, and many other data services and databases.

Types of modems

There are two basic types of modems—the external desktop and the internal. Each type has some advantages and disadvantages.

External   External modems require some of your precious desk space and a voltage source. It also requires a COM port to drive it. The good news is that most external models have LEDs that light up and let you know what is happening during your call.

Both external and the internal models have speakers that allow you to hear the phone ringing or if you get a busy signal. Some external models have a volume control for the built-in speaker.

Internal   Internal modems are built entirely on a board, usually a half or short board. The good news is that they don't use up any of your desk space. The bad news is that they use one of your precious slots. Also, internal modems do not have LEDs to let you know the progress of your call. Even if you use an external modem, if your motherboard does not have built-in COM ports, you will need an I/O board and you will have to use one of your slots for a COM port.

Communications software

A modem is driven and controlled by software. There are dozens of communication programs that can be used. Crosstalk was one earlier modem program. They now have a Crosstalk for Windows version. It works with any version of Windows, which makes it very easy to learn and use.

ProComm is one of several low-cost shareware programs. In many areas it might outperform some of the high-cost commercial programs. The registration cost is $89.

Qmodem is another excellent shareware program that is available for a registration cost of only $30. It is now a part of Mustang Software. This company has developed a bulletin board software program that is very good. If you would like to set up your own bulletin board, give them a call.

You can get copies of shareware programs from bulletin boards or from any of the several companies that provide public domain software. Shareware is not free. You can try it out and use it, but the developers ask that you register the program and send in a nominal sum. For this low cost, they will usually provide a manual and some support.

Hayes compatibility

One of the most popular early modems was made by Hayes Microcomputer Products. They are the IBM of the modem world and have established a de facto standard. There are hundreds of modem manufacturers. Except for some of the very inexpensive ones, almost all of them emulate the Hayes standard.

Protocols

Protocols are procedures that have been established for exchanging data, along with the instructions that coordinate the process. Most protocols can sense when the data is corrupted or lost due to noise, static, or a bad connection. They will automatically resend the affected data until it is received correctly.

There are several protocols, but the most popular ones are Kermit (named for Kermit the frog), Xmodem, and Ymodem. These protocols transmit a block of data along with an error-checking code. They then wait for the receiver to send back an acknowledgment before sending another block. Noise and static are in the form of alternating voltage. A bit of static can easily corrupt a file that is being sent. If a block does not get through, it is re-sent immediately.

Protocols such as Zmodem and HyperProtocol send a whole file in a continuous stream of data with error-checking codes instead of certain intervals. They then wait for confirmation of a successful transmission. If the transmission is unsuccessful, the whole file must be re-sent. The sending and receiving modems should both use the same protocol.

CCITT recommended standards

The communications industry is very complex. There are many different manufacturers and software developers. Each of them wants to differentiate their hardware or software by adding new features, so there have not been many real standards. You might have difficulties if you want to communicate with someone else who is not using the same features.

A United Nations committee has helped to establish some standards. It is called the Comite Consulatif Internal de Telegrahique et Telephone (CCITT). This committee has representatives from over 80 countries and several large private manufacturers. The committee makes recommendations only. A company is free to use or ignore them, but more and more companies are now adopting the recommendations.

All CCITT recommendations for small computers have a V or X prefix. The V series is for use with switched telephone networks, which is almost all of them. The X series is for systems that do not use switched phone lines. Revisions or alternate recommendations have bis (second) or ter (third) added. Here are a few CCITT recommendations:

- **V.22**—a 1200 baud standard.
- **V.22 bis**—a 2400 baud standard.
- **V.32**—a 9600 baud standard.
- **V.42**—an error correcting protocol that includes MNP-4 and LAP M error correction.
- **V.42 bis**—a standard for 4:1 data compression. Under ideal conditions, this standard could permit data transmission speed four times greater than the rated baud rate. With this much compression a 9600 bps modem could transmit 38,400 bps. A 14.4K can transmit at 57.6K.
- **X.25**—a protocol for packet mode communications on data networks such as Telenet and Tymnet.
- **MNP**—Microcom networking protocol which is a series of 10 different protocols developed by the Microcom company. Several of their protocols are very similar to the CCITT V series.
- **LAP M and LAP B**—other protocols that are supported by AT&T and Hayes. They are similar to the CCITT V.42 error correcting standard.

Baud rate

Telephone systems were originally designed for voice and have a very narrow bandwidth. They are subject to noise, static, and other electrical disturbances. These problems and the state of technology at the time limited original modems to about five characters per second (cps), or a rate of 50 baud.

The term *baud* comes from Emile Baudot (1845–1903), a French inventor. Originally, the baud rate was a measure of the dots and dashes in telegraphy. It is now defined as the actual rate of symbols transmitted per second. For the lower baud rates, it is essentially the same as bits per second. Remember that it takes eight bits to make a character. Just as we have periods and spaces to separate words, we must use one *start bit* and two *stop bits* to separate the on/off bits into characters. A transmission of 300 baud means that 300 on/off bits are sent in 1 second. Counting the start/stop bits, it takes 11 bits for each character. So 300 divided by 11 gives about 27 cps.

Some of the newer technologies might actually transmit symbols that represent more than one bit. For baud rates of 1200 and higher, the cps and baud rate can be considerably different.

There have been some fantastic advances in modem technologies. Most modems today operate at 2400 baud, but many are sold that operate at 9600 and 14.4K baud. The 14.4K baud rate, along with the V.42 compression ratio of 4:1 will become the standard. Using the 4:1 compression allows a transmission rate of 57.6K baud.

When communicating with another modem , both the sending and receiving unit must operate at the same baud rate and use the same protocols. Most of the faster modems are downward compatible and can operate at slower speeds.

Ordinarily, the higher the baud rate, the less time it takes to download or transmit a file. (This might not always be, because at the higher speeds, more transmission errors might be encountered. In case of errors, parts of the file or the whole file might have to be retransmitted.) If the file is being sent over a long-distance line, the length of telephone connect time can be costly. If your modem is used frequently, your telephone bills could be very substantial, especially if you have a slow modem.

How to estimate connect time

You can figure the approximate length of time it will take to transmit a file. For rough approximations of cps you can divide the baud rate by 10. For instance, 1200 would be 120 cps, 2400 would be 240 cps. Look at the directory and determine the number of bytes in the file. Divide the number of bytes in the file by the cps. Then multiply that figure by 1.3 for the start/stop bits to get a final approximation. For instance, with a 1200 baud modem and a 40K file, divide 40K by 120 cps to get 333 seconds times 1.3 equals about 433 seconds or 7.2 minutes. If you transmitted the same 40K file with a 2400 baud modem, it would be 40,000/240=167×1.3=217 seconds or 3.6 minutes. With a 9600 baud modem, the same 40K file could be sent in about 55 seconds.

What to buy

What you buy will depend on what you want to do and how much you want to spend. There are hundreds of modem manufacturers, each having models with different functions and prices.

Considering the telephone rates for long distance, if you expect to do much communicating with a modem, it might be worthwhile to spend a bit more and buy a high-speed modem. Look in any computer magazine and you will see dozens of ads for modems. Most of them are fairly close in quality and function.

One company that I want to mention is US Robotics. They manufacture a large variety of modems, especially the high-end high-speed type. They will send you a free 110-page booklet that explains all you need to know about modems.

Installing a modem

If you are adding a modem on a board to a system that is already assembled, the first thing to do is to remove the computer cover. Find an empty slot and plug it in.

Set configuration Before the modem board is plugged into the slot on the motherboard, it will have to be set or configured to access either serial port COM1 or COM2. The board will have jumpers or small switches that must be set to enable either COM1 or COM2.

If you are installing an external modem, you must go through the same procedure to make sure the COM port is accessible and does not conflict. If you have a mouse, serial printer, or other serial device, you will have to determine which port they are set to. You cannot have two serial devices set to the same COM port.

Plug in the board and hook it up to the telephone line. Unless you expect to do a lot of communicating, you probably will not need a separate dedicated line. Your modem might have an automatic answer mode. In this mode it will always answer the telephone. Unless you have a dedicated line, this mode should be disabled. Check your documentation; there should be a switch or some means to disable it.

Plug in telephone line Having the modem and telephone on the same line should cause no problems unless someone tries to use the telephone while the modem is using it. If you are going to be using the modem extensively, or if you have a fax, then you might want to consider getting a separate dedicated line.

There should be two connectors at the back of the board. One might be labeled for the line in and the other for the telephone. Unless you have a dedicated telephone line, you should unplug your telephone, plug the line into the modem, and plug the telephone into the modem. If your computer is not near your telephone line, you might have to go to a hardware store and buy a long telephone extension line.

A simple modem test After you have connected all of the lines, turn on your computer and try the modem before you put the cover back on. Make sure you have software. Call a local bulletin board. Even if you can't get through, or have a wrong number, you should hear the dial tone and hear it dial the number.

It is often difficult to determine which COM port is being used by a device. You can use the AT command to determine if your modem is working. At the DOS prompt C:>, type ECHO AT DT12345>COM1:. If the modem is set properly, you will hear a dial tone, then the modem will dial 12345. If two devices are set for COM1 there will be a conflict. The computer will try for a while, then give an error message and the familiar, Abort, Retry, Ignore, Fail? If there is nothing attached to the port, you might get no message. A shareware program that can check your serial ports or let you use COM3 and COM4 is Port Finder ((713) 462-7687).

Cables An external modem is connected to one of the COM ports with a cable. If you did not get a cable with your unit, you will have to buy one. If you have built-in

COM ports, the cable will cost about $5. If you have to use the bus to access the ports, you will need a cable and an I/O board with serial ports.

Bulletin boards

There are more than 100 bulletin boards in the San Francisco Bay area and about twice that many in the Los Angeles area. Some of them are free of charge. You only have to pay the phone bill if they are out of your calling area. Some bulletin boards charge a nominal fee to join, and some just ask for a tax-deductible donation.

Some bulletin boards are set up by private individuals and some by companies and vendors as a service to their customers. Some are set up by user groups and other special-interest organizations. There are more than 100 bulletin boards nationwide that have been set up for doctors and lawyers.

Most of the bulletin boards are set up to help individuals. They usually have lots of public domain software and a space where you can leave messages for help, to advertise something for sale or for just plain chitchat.

If you are just getting started, you probably need some software. Public domain software packages are available that are as good as major programs. And the best part is that they are free. Good shareware programs are also available.

Viruses and Trojan horses

There have been reports of "viruses" in some public and commercial software. Sick software appears to work as it should, but eventually, it contaminates and destroys many files. The viruses often cause the files to grow in size.

Trojan horses usually do not contaminate other files. They lie dormant for a certain length of time or until a program has been run a certain number of times, and then it destroys the files. Some commercial software is sold with a system that is somewhat similar to a Trojan horse. The buyer pays to use the program a certain number of times, and after that, it will no longer operate.

If you download bulletin board software, it is probably best to run it from a floppy disk until you are sure it is not sick. Before using the program, run an anti-virus program. Several companies have developed software to detect viruses, but it is almost impossible to detect them all. A good shareware program is McAfee Scan program. It is available from several shareware companies or from the BBS at (408) 988-4004.

Illegal activities

Some bulletin boards have been used for illegal and criminal activities. Stolen credit card numbers and telephone charge numbers have been left on the bulletin boards. Consequently, many system operators are now checking any software that is uploaded onto their systems. Many of them restrict access to their boards. Some system operators have begun to start charging a fee because of the extra time it takes to monitor the boards.

Where to find bulletin boards

Check your local computer magazines for bulletin boards and user groups. In California, *MicroTimes* and *Computer Currents* have several pages of bulletin boards and user groups each month. *Computer Shopper* has the most comprehensive listing of bulletin boards and user groups of any national magazine.

On-line services

There are several large national bulletin boards; information and reference services such as CompuServe, Dataquest, Dow Jones, and Dialog. These companies have huge databases of information. A caller can search the databases and download information as easily as pulling the data off his own hard disk. The companies charge a fee for the connect time.

Prodigy is unlike other on-line services. Prodigy does not charge for connect time. They charge only a very nominal monthly rate. They have phone service to most areas in large cities, so for most people, there is no telephone charge. They have an impressive list of services including home shopping, home banking, airline schedules and reservations, stock market quotations, and many others. One of the faults of Prodigy is that it is relatively slow. But because it is so inexpensive, I can live with it.

CompuServe, Delphi, and Genie are major on-line services that are now offering about the same type of shopping that Prodigy offers.

E-mail

Many national bulletin boards offer electronic mail or (E-mail) along with their other services. These services can be of great value to some individuals and businesses.

E-mail subscribers are usually given a "post office box" at these companies. This is usually a file on one of their large hard-disk systems. When a message is received, it is recorded in this file. The next time the subscriber logs on to the service, he or she is alerted that there is "mail" in their box.

E-mail is becoming more popular everyday and there are now several hundred thousand subscribers. The cost for an average message is about $1. The cost for overnight mail from the U.S. Post Office, Federal Express, and UPS is $11 to $13. Some companies that provide E-mail include:

- AT&T Mail   (800) 367-7225
- CompuServe   (800) 848-8990
- DASne   (408) 559-7434
- MCI Mail   (800) 444-6245
- Western Union (800) 527-5184

Banking by modem

Many banks offer systems that let you do all your banking with your computer and a modem from the comforts of your home. You will never again have to drive downtown, hunt for a parking space, and stand in line for a half hour to do your banking.

Public domain and shareware

If you don't have a modem yet, or if the local bulletin boards don't have the software you need, there are several companies that will ship you public domain and shareware software on a floppy diskette. These companies have thousands of programs and usually charge from $3 up to $24 for a disk full of programs. There are several public domain software companies. Most of them advertise in the computer magazines listed in chapter 15.

ISDN

ISDN is an acronym for integrated services digital network. Eventually the whole world will have telephone systems that use this concept. It is a system that is able to transmit voice, data, video, and graphics in digital form rather than the present analog form. When this happens, you can scrap your modem. You will need only a simple interface to communicate.

ISDN is already installed in several cities. It was scheduled to be fully implemented in the U.S. by 1992, but don't hold your breath waiting for it. The service might not be available at all locations for some time, so don't throw your modem away just yet.

Facsimile boards and machines

Facsimile (fax) machines have been around for quite a while. Newspapers and businesses have used them for years. They were the forerunners of scanning machines. The early machines were similar to the early acoustic modems. Both used foam rubber cups that fit over the telephone receiver and mouthpiece for coupling. They were very slow and subject to noise and interference. Fax machines and modems have come a long way since those early days.

A page of text or a photo is fed into the facsimile machine and scanned. As the scanning beam moves across the page, white and dark areas are digitized as 1s and 0s, which are then transmitted over the telephone lines.

Modems and facsimile machines are quite similar and are related in many respects. A modem sends and receives bits of data. A fax machine or board usually sends and receives scanned, whole-page letters, images, signatures, etc. A computer program can be sent over a modem, but not over a fax. A fax sends and receives the information as digitized data.

Millions of facsimile machines are in use today. Many businesses benefit from the use of fax machines. They can be used to send documents, signatures, seals, letterheads, graphs, blueprints, photos, and other types of data around the world, across the country, or across the room to another fax machine.

It costs from $8.50 to $13 to send an overnight letter. E-mail can send the same letter for $1. A fax machine can deliver it for about 40 cents and can do it in less than 3 minutes. Depending on the type of business and the amount of critical mail that must be sent out, a fax system can pay for itself in a very short time.

Stand-alone fax units

Facsimile machines were once stand-alone devices that attached to a telephone. They have been vastly improved in the last few years. Most of them are as easy to use as a copy machine. In fact, most of them can be used as a copy machine.

Some overseas companies are making stand-alone units that are fairly inexpensive, some for as little as $400. You might not be happy with a low-cost machine, however. You might be better off to spend a bit more and get one with features such as a paper cutter, high resolution, voice/data switch on the system, document feeder, automatic dialer, automatic retry, delayed transmission, transmission confirmation, polling, built-in laser printer, large memory, and uses plain paper. You might not need or be able to afford all of these features, but try to get a machine with as many as possible. Of course, the more features, the higher the cost.

Fax computer boards

Several companies have developed fax machines on circuit boards that can be plugged into computers. Many of the newer models have provisions for a modem on the same board. Follow the same procedure to install a fax board as outlined previously for installing an internal modem.

Special software allows the computer to control the fax board. Using the computer's word processor, letters and memos can be written and sent over the phone lines. Several letters or other information can be stored or retrieved from the computer hard disk and transmitted. The computer can even be programmed to send the letters out at night when the rates are lower.

Computer fax boards have one disadvantage. They cannot scan information unless there is a scanner attached to the computer. Without a scanner, the information that can be sent is usually limited to what can be entered from a keyboard or disk. As I pointed out before, stand-alone units scan pages of information, including such things as handwriting, signatures, images, blueprints, and photos. It is fairly easy to attach a scanner to your computer. Scanners are discussed in chapter 9.

Fax boards can cost $100 up to $1000, depending on the extras and goodies installed. Pay close attention to the ads and specifications. I have seen several fax boards advertised for less than $100. The reason for the low cost is that these boards will send fax files, but they are unable to receive them. Nowhere in the ad did it mention this fact. Even when I called one company, they were reluctant to admit that their boards only worked in the send mode. The reason they can sell them for less is because it requires more electronics to receive a fax than it does to send. For a boiler-room type of operation that does nothing but send out ads, this board would probably be sufficient.

Single-board modem and fax

I have an Intel Connection coprocessor. It is a sophisticated fax board with its own 10-MHz 80188 processor. It has provisions for a small daughter board that contains a 2400 baud modem. Because it has its own processor, it can send and receive fax messages or operate the modem in the background while the computer is busy on other projects. My Intel Connection coprocessor is about 3 years old. They have since developed a newer and better system called the SatisFAXtion. There are several other vendors who offer fax boards and combination modems. Check the computer magazine ads.

Installing a fax board

Most fax boards are very easy to install and operate. If your computer is already assembled, remove the screws that hold the cover on. Check your documentation and set any switches necessary, then plug the board into an empty slot. Replace the cover and connect the telephone line.

You should have received some software needed to control the fax. This software should be installed on your hard disk. You should then be up and ready to send and receive faxes.

If you use a word processing program, such as WordStar, to create letters or text for a fax transmission, the text must be changed into an ASCII file before it can be sent. Most word processors have this capability.

Chapter 11

Monitors

Most of the time spent working on a computer will be spent looking at the monitor. You can buy a monochrome monitor for as little as $65. This might be sufficient for what you have to do. But life can be a lot more enjoyable if you have a good, high-resolution color monitor. Even if you do nothing but word processing, color makes the job a lot more pleasant. But color costs, and like so many other things in life, the better the color and the higher the resolution, the higher the cost. Also, the larger the screen, the higher the cost.

There have been several improvements in the design and development of monitor electronics. New chip sets and VLSI integration have helped reduce the cost of manufacturing many electronics. Not much can be done to reduce the cost of manufacturing the main component, the cathode-ray tube (CRT). A good color CRT requires a tremendous amount of labor-intensive, precision work. The larger the screen, the more costly it is to manufacture.

We are very fortunate in that there are many different manufacturers. They make many different types, sizes, and kinds of monitors, and this competition helps to keep the prices fairly reasonable.

Available options

Because there are so many types of monitors and so many options, you will have some difficult decisions to make when you buy your system. You will have a very wide choice as to price, resolution, color, size, and shape. As I mentioned before, you can buy a 12-inch monochrome monitor for as little as $65. Color VGA and Super VGA might cost $200 and more. The average price for a good 14-inch VGA monitor is about $300. The brand-name models, such as NEC, will cost more.

The monitor is a critical part of your system, and it can represent a large percentage of the cost of a system. For this reason you should make sure that you get the best that you can afford. If you are buying by mail, or even at a store, try to get a copy of the manufacturer's specifications and study them. Look at the ads in computer magazines to get an idea of monitor costs. But be aware that ads cost a lot of money, so a lot of good information is sometimes left out. Call the vendor and ask for a specification sheet.

Monitor basics

I am going to discuss monitor specifications, terms, and acronyms so that you can make a more informed decision as to which monitor to buy. Basically a monitor is similar to a television set. The face of a TV set or a monitor is the end of a cathode-ray tube (CRT). CRTs are vacuum tubes and they have many of the same elements that made up the old vacuum tubes that were used before the advent of the semiconductor age. CRTs have a filament that boils off a stream of electrons. The back of the CRT screen has a voltage potential of about 25,000 volts, creating a very strong attraction for the electrons that are boiled off the cathode. The electrons are "shot" from an electron gun toward the back of the CRT screen where they slam into the phosphor and cause it to light up. The electron beam moves rapidly across the screen, and because the phosphor continues to glow for awhile, we see the images that are created.

When we watch a movie, we are seeing a series of still photos, flashed one after the other. Due to our persistence of vision, it appears to be continuous motion. It is this same persistence of vision that allows us to see motion and images on our television and video screens.

In a magnetic field, a beam of electrons acts very much like a piece of iron. Just like iron, a stream of electrons can be attracted or repelled by the polarity of a magnet. In a CRT, a beam of electrons must pass between a system of electromagnets before it reaches the back of the CRT face. In a basic system there is an electromagnet on the left, one on the right, one at the top, and one at the bottom. Voltage through the electromagnets is varied so that the beam of electrons is repelled by one side and attracted by the other, or pulled to the top or forced to the bottom. With this electromagnetic system, a stream of electrons can be bent and directed to any spot on the screen. It is much like holding a hose and directing a high-pressure stream of water to an area.

Scan rates

When you look at the screen of a TV set or a monitor, you see a full screen only because of the persistence of vision and the type of phosphor used on the back of the screen. Actually, the beam of electrons starts at the top left corner of the screen, and under the influence of the electromagnets, it is pulled across to the top right-hand corner. It lights up the pixels as it sweeps across. It is then returned to the left-hand side, dropped down one line, and swept across again. On a TV set, this is repeated so that 525 lines are written on the screen in about ⅙₀ of a second. This is one frame, so 60 frames are written to the screen in 1 second.

Vertical scan rate

The time that it takes to fill a screen with lines from top to bottom is the *vertical scan rate*. Some newer multiscan, or multifrequency, monitors have variable vertical scan rates from 40 times per second to 100 times per second.

Horizontal scan rate

The horizontal scanning frequency of a standard TV set is 15.75 kHz. This is also the frequency used by CGA systems. Higher resolutions require higher frequencies. The horizontal frequency for an EGA system is about 22 kHz, and for VGA is 31.5 kHz and up. Multiscan or multisync monitors can accept various frequencies sent to them from the adapter card. They can accept horizontal signals from 15.5 kHz to 100 kHz. Some of the older software was written specifically for CGA, EGA, or VGA systems. Multiscan can run any of them.

Some of the low-cost monitors might accept only two or three fixed frequencies, such as the 15.75 kHz for CGA, 22 kHz for EGA, and 31.5 kHz for VGA. Depending on your needs and bank account, this might be all you need. But multiscanning is better if you can afford it.

Controlling the beam

The CRT has control grids, much like the old vacuum tubes, for controlling the signal. A small signal voltage applied to the grid can control a very large voltage. The control grid, along with the electromagnetic system, controls the electron stream. It causes it to make a large voltage output copy the small input signal. This amplified high voltage is then used to write a replica of the input signal on the screen. As the beam sweeps across the screen, if the input signal is tracing the outline of a figure, the control grid will turn the beam on to light up a dot of phosphor for the light areas. If the input signal is of a dark area, the beam is shut off so that a portion of the screen will be dark for that area of the image.

Monochrome

A monochrome monitor has a single electron gun and a single color phosphor. It writes directly on the phosphor and can provide very high resolution for text and graphics. It is even possible to get monochrome analog VGA, which can display in as many as 64 different shades. Large monochrome monitors might be ideal for some desktop publishing (DTP) systems and even some CAD systems, but these large monochrome monitors can be almost as expensive as the equivalent size in color.

Color

Color TVs and monitors are much more complicated than monochrome systems. During the manufacture of color monitors, three different phosphors—red, green, and blue—are deposited on the back of the screen. Usually a very small dot of each color is placed in a triangular shape. They have three electron guns, one for each color. By lighting up the three different colored phosphors selectively, all the colors of the rainbow can be generated.

The guns are called red, green, and blue (RGB), but the electrons they emit are all the same. They are called RGB because each gun is aimed so that it hits a red, a green, or blue color on the back of the monitor screen. They are very accurately aimed so that they will converge or impinge only on their assigned color.

Resolution

If you look closely at a black-and-white photo in a newspaper, you can see that the photo is made up of small dots. There are a lot of dots in the darker areas and fewer in the light areas. The text or image on a monitor or a television screen is also made up of dots very similar to those in a newspaper photo. You can easily see these dots with a magnifying glass. If you look closely, you can see spaces between the dots. This is much like the dots of a dot matrix printer. The more dots and the closer together they are, the better the resolution. A good high-resolution monitor will have solid, sharply defined characters and images. An ideal resolution would look very much like a high-quality photograph. But it will be some time before we reach the resolution of film.

Pixels

Resolution is determined by the number of picture elements, or pixels, that can be displayed. The following figures relate primarily to text, but the graphics resolution is similar. A standard CGA monitor can display 640×200 pixels. It can display 80 characters in one line with 25 lines from top to bottom. If you divide 640 by 80, you find that one character will be 8 pixels wide. There can be 25 lines of characters, so $200/25 = 8$ pixels high. The entire screen has $640 \times 200 = 128,000$ pixels.

Most monitor adapters have text character generators built onto the board. When you send an A to the screen, the adapter goes to its library and sends the signal for the preformed A to the screen. Each character occupies a cell made up of the appropriate number of pixels depending on the resolution of the screen and the adapter. In the case of the CGA monitor, if all the dots within a cell were lit up, there would be a solid block of dots 8 pixels wide and 8 pixels high. When the A is placed in a cell, only the dots necessary to form the outline of an A are lit up. It is very similar to the dots formed by the dot matrix printer when it prints a character.

An EGA monitor can display 640×350, or $640/80 = 8$ pixels wide and $350/25 = 14$ pixels high. The screen can display $640 \times 350 = 224,000$ total pixels. Enhanced EGA and VGA can display $640 \times 480 = 307,200$ total pixels; 8 pixels wide and 19 pixels high.

Standards

The Video Electronics Standards Association (VESA) has chosen 800×600 to be the Super VGA standard, which is $800/80 = 10$ pixels wide and $600/25 = 24$ pixels high. Many newer systems are now capable of 1024×768, 1280×1024, 1664×1200, and more. With a resolution of 1664×1200, you would have 1,996,800 pixels or almost 2 million pixels that could be lit up. We have come a long way from the 128,000 pixels possible with CGA. IBM has proposed that XGA be a new standard. It would have a resolution of 1024×768 and a vertical scan rate (refresh rate) of 70 Hz.

The need for drivers and high-resolution programs

You should be aware that even if you have a possible resolution of 1664×1200, your monitor will not display it unless you are using a driver or program that calls for it. If you are doing word processing or running an older program, your monitor will probably be displaying at 640×480 or even less.

Interlaced versus noninterlaced

The VGA horizontal system sweeps the electron beam across the screen from top to bottom 480 times in $\frac{1}{60}$ of a second to make one frame, or 60 frames in 1 second. For Super VGA, it sweeps 600 times, and for XGA, it sweeps 768 times in $\frac{1}{60}$ of a second. Clearly, the higher the resolution, the more lines there are, the closer they are together, and the faster they have to be painted on the screen. The higher resolution also causes the electron beam to light up more pixels on each line as it sweeps across.

Higher horizontal frequencies demand more precise and higher-quality electronics, which of course, requires higher costs to manufacture. To avoid this higher cost, IBM designed some of their VGA systems with an interlaced horizontal system. Instead of increasing the horizontal frequency, they paint every other line across the screen from top to bottom, then return to the top and paint the lines that were skipped. Theoretically, this sounds like a great idea. But practically, it doesn't work too well because it causes a flicker that can be very irritating to some people who have to work with this type of monitor for very long.

This flicker might not be readily apparent, but some people have complained of eyestrain, headaches, and fatigue after prolonged use of an interlaced monitor. If the head is turned slightly sideways, you might see it in the corner of your eye along the edges of the screen. It might be more noticeable when doing intensive graphics. If the monitor is only used for short periods of time, the flicker might not be noticeable.

Some companies make models that use interlacing in certain modes, but the same model might use noninterlacing in other modes. Most companies don't advertise the fact that their monitors use interlacing. The interlace models are usually a bit lower in price than the noninterlaced models. Many of them also use the IBM standard 8514 chip set. You might have to ask the vendor what system is used.

There are other companies besides IBM that make interlaced monitors. If you get a chance, compare the interlaced and noninterlaced types. You might not be able to tell the difference. If cost is a prime consideration, the interlaced type is usually a bit less expensive.

The adapter you buy should match your monitor. Use an interlaced adapter with an interlaced monitor. An adapter that can send only interlaced signals might not work with a noninterlaced monitor. Some adapters are able to adjust and operate with both interlaced and noninterlaced monitors.

Dot pitch

The distance between the dots is called the *dot pitch*. The dots per inch determines the resolution. A high-resolution monitor might have a dot pitch of 0.31 millimeter (mm). (1 mm = 0.0394 inch, 0.31 mm = 0.0122 inch or about the thickness of an average business card.) A typical medium-resolution monitor might have a dot pitch of 0.39 mm. One with very high resolution might have a dot pitch of 0.26 mm or even less. The smaller the dot pitch, the more precise and more difficult the monitor is to manufacture.

The size of the monitor makes a difference in dot pitch. A 0.31-mm dot pitch would be okay for a 20-inch monitor, but it would not be very good for a 12-inch one. Some of the low-cost monitors have a dot pitch of 0.42 mm to as great as 0.52 mm. A 0.52-mm dot pitch might be suitable for playing some games, but it would be difficult to do any productive computing on such a system.

Landscape versus portrait

Most monitors are wider than they are tall. These are called landscape styles. There are others that are taller than they are wide. These are called portrait styles. Portrait style monitors are often used for desktop publishing and other special applications.

Adapter basics

It won't do you much good to buy a high-resolution monitor unless you buy a good adapter to drive it. You can't just plug a monitor into your computer and expect it to function. Just as a hard disk needs a controller, a monitor needs an adapter to interface with the computer. Like the hard disk manufacturers, many of the monitor manufacturers do not make adapter boards. Just as a hard disk can operate with several different types of controllers, most monitors can operate with several different types of adapters. The monitor and adapter should be fairly well matched. It is possible to buy an adapter that has greater capabilities than the monitor can respond to, or your monitor might be capable of greater resolution than the adapter can supply.

The original IBM PC came with a green monochrome monitor and a monochrome display adapter (MDA) that could display text only. The Hercules company immediately saw the folly of this limitation, so they developed the Hercules monographic adapter (HMGA) and set a new standard. It wasn't long before IBM and a lot of other companies were selling similar MGA cards that could display both graphics and text. These adapters provide a high resolution of 720×350 on monochrome monitors.

IBM then introduced their color monitor and color graphics adapter (CGA). It provides only 640×200 resolution. The CGA is a digital system that allows a mix of red, green, and blue. The cables have four lines, one each for red, green, and blue, and one for intensity. This allows two different intensities for each color—on for bright and off for dim. So there are four objects, each of which can be in either of two states, or two to the fourth power ($2^4 = 16$); therefore, CGA has a limit of 16 colors. CGA monitors have very large spaces between pixels so that the resolution and color are terrible.

An enhanced graphics adapter (EGA) can drive a high-resolution monitor to display 640×350 resolution. Super EGA can display 640×480. The EGA system has six lines and allows each of the primary colors to be mixed together in any of four different intensities, so there are 2^6 or 64 different colors that can be displayed.

The CGA system is obsolete. I would not advise anyone to buy one. The EGA system is also nearly obsolete. But just like the obsolete 360K and 720K floppy drives, some vendors are still pushing the CGA and EGA systems. You might be able to find a good buy on an EGA system, and depending on what you want to do with your computer and how much you want to spend, this might be all you need. But for just a few dollars more than the cost of an EGA system, you can buy a much better VGA system.

Analog versus digital

Up until the introduction of the PS/2 with VGA, most displays used the digital system. But digital systems have severe limitations. Digital signals are of two states, either on or off. The signals for color and intensity require separate lines in the cables. As pointed out earlier, it takes six lines for the EGA to display 16 colors out of a palette of 64.

The analog signals that drive the color guns are voltages that are continuously variable. It takes only a few lines for the three primary colors. The intensity voltage for each color can then be varied almost infinitely to create as many as 256 colors out of a possible 262,144.

Digital systems are sometimes called TTL (transistor to transistor logic). Some monitors that can handle both digital and analog might have a switch that says TTL for the digital mode.

11-1 A video graphics adapter.

Very high-resolution graphics adapters

Many of the high-resolution adapters have 1Mb or more of video RAM (VRAM) on board. Some adapter boards are sold with only 512K of VRAM. They usually have empty sockets for another 512K. You can buy VRAM and install it yourself. VRAM is about the same price as DRAM. Figure 11-1 shows a high-resolution adapter with 1MB of VRAM on the left portion of the board. It has empty sockets for another 1MB.

A single complex graphics image might require more than 1Mb of memory to store. By having the memory on the adapter board, it saves having to go through the bus to the conventional RAM. Some adapter boards even have separate plug-in daughterboards for extra memory. Many of them, such as the Texas Instruments 34010 or the Hitachi HD63483, have their own coprocessor on board.

Depending on the resolution capabilities and the goodies that it has, a very high-resolution adapter board might cost from $150 to $3400. The high-resolution adapters are downward compatible. If you run a program that was designed for CGA, it will be displayed in CGA format even though you have a very high-resolution monitor, but it will look a lot better than it would on a CGA monitor.

Bandwidth

The bandwidth of a monitor is the range of frequencies that its circuits can handle. A multiscan monitor can accept horizontal frequencies from 15.75 kHz to about 40 kHz and vertical frequencies from 40 Hz to about 90 Hz. To get a rough estimate of the bandwidth required, multiply the resolution pixels times the vertical scan or frame rate. For instance, a Super VGA or VESA standard monitor should have $800 \times 600 \times 60$ Hz = 28.8 MHz. However, the systems require a certain amount of overhead, such as for retrace (the time needed to move back to the left side of the screen, drop down one line, and start a new line), so the bandwidth should be at least 30 MHz. If the vertical scan rate is 90 Hz, then it is $800 \times 600 \times 90$ = 43.2 MHz, or at least 45 MHz. A very high-resolution monitor would require a bandwidth of $1600 \times 1200 \times 90$ = 172.8 MHz, or about 180 MHz counting the overhead. Many of the very high-resolution units are specified at 200-MHz video bandwidth. Of course, the higher the bandwidth, the more costly and difficult the monitor is to manufacture.

Drivers

Be sure to ask your vendor about drivers for the adapter that you buy. Without the drivers you might not be able to fully utilize the high resolution of your system. Most new software being developed today has built-in hooks that allow them to take advantage of the high-resolution goodies. Older software programs written before EGA and VGA were developed, normally cannot take advantage of the higher resolution and extended graphics.

Most manufacturers supply software drivers with their adapters for programs such as Windows, Lotus, AutoCAD, GEM, Ventura, WordStar, and others. Some vendors supply as many as two or three diskettes full of drivers. Depending on what software you intend to use, the drivers supplied with the adapter you purchase might be an important consideration.

Screen size

The stated screen size is measured diagonally, the same as a television screen is measured. There is usually an unusable border area on all four sides of the screen. The usable viewing area on my 13-inch NEC is about 9.75 inches wide and about 7.75 inches high. One reason is because the screen is markedly curved near the edges. This curve can cause distortion so the areas are masked off and not used.

For some types of CAD work or desktop publishing, it would be helpful to have a bigger screen. But prices go up almost at a logarithmic rate for sizes above 14 inches. A 14-inch monitor might cost less than $500, a 16-inch one might cost about $1200, and a 19- or 20-inch one might cost $2500 or more. The size monitor that you should buy depends on what you want to do with your computer and how much money you want to spend.

Controls

Controls adjust the brightness, contrast, and vertical/horizontal lines. Some manufacturers place the controls on the back of the monitor or in other areas that are difficult to get to. It is much better if they are accessible from the front or side so that you can see what the effect is as you adjust them.

Glare

If a monitor reflects too much light, it can be like a mirror and be very distracting. Some manufacturers coat their screens with a silicon formula to reduce the reflectance. Some etch the screen for the same purpose. Some screens are tinted to help cut down on glare. If possible, you should try the monitor under various lighting conditions. If you have a glare problem, several supply companies and mail-order houses offer glare shields from $20 to $100.

Cleaning the screen

Because there are about 25,000 volts of electricity hitting the back of the monitor face, it creates a static attraction for dust. This can distort the image and make the screen difficult to read. Most manufacturers provide an instruction booklet that suggests how their screen should be cleaned. If you have a screen that has been coated with silicon to reduce glare, you should not use any harsh cleansers on it. In most cases, plain water and a soft paper towel will work fine.

Tilt and swivel base

Most people place their monitor on top of their computer. If you are short or tall, have a low or high chair, or have a nonstandard size desk, the monitor might not be at eye level. A tilt and swivel base allows you to position the monitor to best suit you. Many monitors now come with this base. If yours does not have one, many specialty stores and mail-order houses sell them for $15 to $40.

Several supply and mail-order houses also offer an adjustable arm that clamps to the desk and has a small platform for the monitor to sit on. The arm can swing up and down and from side to side. This can free a lot of desk space. These adjustable platforms cost from $50 to $150.

Cables

Some monitors do not come with cables, and vendors sell them separately for an additional $25 to $75. Even monitors that have cables might not have the type of connectors to fit your adapter. At this time, there is little or no standardization for cable and adapter connectors. Make sure that you get the proper cables to match your adapter and monitor.

Monitor and adapter sources

I have worked with many monitors in my lifetime, but there are hundreds that I have not had the chance to personally evaluate. I subscribe to *PC Week, Byte, PC Sources, InfoWorld, PC World, Computer Shopper, Computer Monthly,* and about 50 other computer magazines. Most of these magazines have test labs that do extensive tests of products for their excellent reviews. Because I can't personally test all of these products, I rely heavily on their reviews. I can't possibly list all of the monitor and adapter vendors. I suggest that you look through the magazines listed above and in chapter 15.

List price versus street price

Note that the prices quoted from manufacturers in most magazine reviews are list prices. Often, the "street price" of the product will be much less. There is a tremendous difference in the list price and the actual price you should pay. Besides, in this volatile market, the prices change almost daily. Call first, if ordering from a magazine ad.

What to buy if you can afford it

The two questions you should ask yourself when choosing a monitor should be, What is it going to be used for? and How much do I want to spend? If money is no object, buy a large 20-inch analog monitor with super high resolution and a good Super VGA board to drive it for about $2000. If money is important, you might consider a system such as the 20-inch Sampo TriSync for about $1000. This system uses three of the most common fixed frequencies.

If you expect to do any graphics, CAD/CAM design work, or close-tolerance designs, you will definitely need a good, large-screen color monitor with very high resolution. A large screen is almost essential for many types of design drawings so that as much of the drawing as possible can be viewed on the screen. It takes a lot of time for the computer to redraw an image on the screen.

For desktop publishing, the very high-resolution monochrome monitors are ideal. They usually can display several shades of gray. Many of these monitors are the portrait type; that is, they are higher than they are wide. Many of them have a display area of 8½ inches by 11 inches. Instead of 25 lines, they have 66 lines, which is the standard for an 11-inch sheet of paper. Many have a phosphor that lets you have black text on a white background so that the screen looks very much like the finished text. Some of the newer color monitors have a mode that lets you switch to pure white with black type. Some of the 19-inch and larger landscape-type monitors (which are wider than they are high) can display two pages of text side by side.

For databases, spreadsheets, accounting, or for word processing, a monochrome monitor is probably sufficient. What should you buy? Buy the biggest and best multiscanning color Super VGA or XGA that you can afford.

A checklist

If at all possible, go to a computer swap meet or to several different stores and compare various models. This might be a good idea even if you are going to buy through mail order. Here are some things that you might want to check:

- **Dot pitch**   Ask for a specification sheet. Check for dot pitch. It should be no less than 0.31 mm for good resolution; 0.28 mm or less is better.
- **Interlacing**   Check for noninterlacing if you expect to do a lot of graphics work.
- **Scan rate**   Check the scan rate—both vertical and horizontal. The less expensive monitors have a fixed rate. Some have two or three fixed rates. The better ones use multiscanning.
- **Bandwidth**   For a rough estimate multiply the resolution times the vertical frequency. For instance, at a vertical frequency of 60 Hz it would be $800 \times 600 \times 60$ Hz = 28.8 MHz, or a minimum of 30 MHz. For a vertical frequency of 70 Hz, it would be $800 \times 600 \times 70$ = 33.6 MHz, or a 35 MHz minimum.
- **Controls**   It is better to have the controls accessible from the front or side. Some manufacturers put them in the back of the monitor. It is very difficult to set up the screen if you can't look at it at the same time.
- **Brightness**   Turn the brightness up and check the center of the screen and the outer edges. The intensity should be the same in the center and edges. Check for glare in different light settings.
- **Applications**   Check the focus, brightness, and contrast with text and with graphics. I have seen some monitors that displayed demonstration graphics programs beautifully, but were terrible when displaying text in various colors.
- **Adapters and drivers**   Try to get an adapter that has as many drivers as possible. Try to get an adapter with a minimum of 1Mb of VRAM, or at least one with 512K of VRAM and the ability to accept 512K more. You can add extra VRAM yourself.
- **Cables**   Make sure you get the proper cables to fit your computer.
- **Tilt and swivel**   Even if you have to pay extra, get a monitor with a tilt and swivel base.

Chapter 12

Printers

Clearly, the type of printer you need will depend on what your computer will be used for. If at all possible, visit a computer store or a computer show before you buy a printer and try it out. Get several spec sheets of printers in your price range and compare. You should also look for reviews of printers in the computer magazines. *PC Magazine* has done an annual printer review every year since 1984. They have excellent test labs and a well-informed review staff. Their reviews and tests are comprehensive, thorough, and unbiased. It is possible to order some of their back issues to check through their reviews.

Dot matrix printers

Most of the dot matrix printers sold today are 24 pins. They are fairly reasonable in price and are sturdy and reliable. The 24-pin printer forms characters from two vertical rows of 12 pins in each row. There are small electric solenoids around each of the wire pins in the head. A signal voltage causes the pins to push forward against the ribbon onto the paper. By pressing various pins as the head moves across the paper, any character can be formed. It is also possible to do some graphics.

Some of the less expensive printers have a vertical row of only 7 or 9 pins. The more expensive ones have 18 or 24 pins. As the head moves in finite increments across the paper, solenoids push individual pins forward to form characters. (Note: The solenoids in a print head generate a powerful magnetic field. Do not place your floppy disk near them while they are printing.)

Figure 12-1 is a representation of the pins in a 7-pin print head and how it would form the letter A. The numbers on the left represent the individual pins in the head before it starts moving across the paper. The first pin to be struck would be number 7, then number 6, then 5, 4, 3, 2, 5, 1, 5, 2, 3, 4, 5, 6, 7.

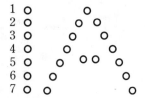

12-1 Pins in a 7-pin print head.

A 24-pin head would be similar to the 7-pin representation above, except that it would have two vertical rows, side by side, of 12 pins in each row. The pins in one row are slightly offset and lower than the pins in the other row. Because the pins are offset, they overlap slightly, filling in the gaps found in 9-pin systems.

Dot matrix speed

In draft mode, the speed can be from 200 cps to 600 cps or more. In near letter quality (NLQ) mode, the speed might be from 60 cps to 330 cps. At 60 cps it would take a little over 1 minute to print a full page of 4000 characters. At 330 cps it would take less than 15 seconds to print a full page, or about 4 pages per minute (ppm).

Dot matrix color

There are some dot matrix printers that use a ribbon with three different stripes of color, usually red, green, and blue. Moving the ribbon up and down causes the head to strike the various colors. They can be overprinted and blended so that all of the colors of the rainbow can be printed. Of course, you need special software to accomplish this. It is a bit slow, but if you need color to jazz up a presentation or for accent now and then, they are great. The color option usually costs about $100 more than standard price.

There are some things that can be done with a dot matrix printer that can't be done with a laser printer. For instance, a dot matrix can have a wide carriage; most lasers are limited to 8½ inches by 11 inches. A dot matrix printer can use continuous sheets or forms; the laser uses cut sheets, fed one at a time. A dot matrix can also print carbons and forms with multiple sheets.

Noise reduction

A dot matrix printer can be very noisy. Enclosures are available that help to reduce the noise, but they are a bit expensive. I put mine on a 2-inch sheet of foam rubber that had been used as packing material. The foam rubber reduces the noise considerably. Some of the newer printers are much quieter.

Low cost

If you can get by with a dot matrix printer, you should be able to find some at very reasonable prices. The low cost of laser printers are forcing down dot matrix prices. In addition to lower prices, many dot matrix companies are also adding features, such as more memory and several fonts in order to attract buyers.

Currently, a good standard carriage, 9-pin dot matrix printer costs as little as $120. A wide carriage 9-pin printer costs about $50 more. A 24-pin standard carriage printer costs about $275, and a wide carriage 24-pin printer costs about $325. Check the ads in the computer magazines.

Head repair

Most dot matrix machines are sturdy and reliable, but as in all mechanical equipment, sometimes they do fail. Often, it is the head that fails. Several companies have repair facilities. One of them is Impact Printhead Services. It is best to get an estimate of the repair costs before having the work done. As with many computer components, it might cost more to repair than to replace.

Label printers

Seiko's Smart Label Plus printer is very small. It sells for about $150. In an office that does a lot of mailing, this might be a good idea. This small printer does nothing but print labels. You can buy a full-featured 9-pin dot matrix for less than the cost of the Seiko Smart Label printer, however. You can print good labels on a 9-pin dot matrix printer, as well as perform other tasks. A disadvantage is that it is a real pain to have to set up the printer each time you want to print a few labels. If you plan to print a lot of labels, you might consider buying a Seiko or a dot matrix and dedicate it solely for labels.

You can also print labels on a laser printer using special labels. Avery Commercial Products produces special labels and software for lasers and other types of printers.

Print buffer

The computer can feed data to a printer much faster than the printer can print it. Most printers have a buffer that can hold from 1K to 50K or more. The data is loaded into the buffer by the computer and it is fed to the printer as needed. With a large buffer, the computer can dump the data, then go about its business doing other things. With a small buffer and a long file, the computer has to sit and load the data into the buffer.

Daisywheel printers

The daisywheel produces excellent letter-quality print. It has a wheel with all the letters of the alphabet on flexible "petals." If the letter A is pressed, an electric solenoid hammer hits the A as it spins by and presses it against a ribbon onto the paper. Daisywheel printers are very slow and cannot print graphics. They are also quite noisy, and are practically obsolete.

Inkjet printers

Dot matrix printers use 9 to 24 pins to impact against a ribbon to create characters or graphics. Inkjet printers use from 30 to 60 small spray nozzles to create characters or graphic images. Most of the inkjet machines print at a 300 DPI resolution, the same as most lasers.

The Hewlett-Packard DeskJet Plus is a small printer that has quality quality almost equal to that of a laser printer. It uses a matrix of small ink jets instead of pins. As the head moves across the paper, the ink is sprayed from the jets to form the letters. It comes with the Courier font, but it can use several other fonts that are available on plug-in cartridges. It has a speed of 1 to 2 pages per minute (PPM). It is small enough to sit on a desktop and is very quiet. It is currently advertised for $549.

Cannon also manufactures printers based on the inkjet technology, but they call it bubble jet. Their BJ-10e is a small portable. It is advertised for $309. Their BJ-130e desktop model is advertised for $647.

The Diconix division of Kodak also makes a small portable inkjet printer. It is advertised for $341. These portables are ideal for attaching to laptops, providing you with excellent letter quality print on the road.

Inkjet color

Hewlett-Packard has two models, the HP PaintJet for 8½ inches by 11 inches and the HP PaintJet XL that can handle paper as large as 11 inches by 17 inches. These printers produce color by using ink cartridges with four different colored inks—black, cyan, yellow, and magenta. They offer a low-cost method for good quality color. A few laser-type color printers rely on a thermal wax transfer method to create color, but they are four to five times more expensive than the inkjet printers. The color inkjet printers are ideal for creating colored transparencies, graphs, schematics, and drawings.

Laser printers

Laser printers have excellent print quality. They are a combination of copy machine, computer, and laser technology. On the down side, they have lots of moving parts and are rather expensive. Laser printers use synchronized, multifaceted mirrors and sophisticated optics to write the characters or images on a photosensitive rotating drum. The drum is similar to the ones used in copy machines. The laser beam is swept across the spinning drum and is turned on and off to represent light and dark areas. As the drum spins, the laser writes one line across the drum, then rapidly returns and writes another. It is quite similar to the electron beam that sweeps across a monitor face one line at a time.

The drum is sensitized by each point of light that hits it. The sensitized areas act like an electromagnet. The drum rotates through the carbon toner and the sensitized areas become covered with toner. The paper is then pressed against the drum and the toner that was picked up by the drum leaves an imprint of the sensitized areas on the paper. Finally, the paper is sent through a heating element where the toner is heated and fused to the paper.

Except for writing to the drum, the process is the same as that which happens in a copy machine. Instead of using a laser to sensitize the drum, a copy machine uses a photographic lens to focus the image onto the rotating drum.

LED and LCS printers

Some companies have developed other systems to write on or sensitize the drum. Some use light-emitting diodes (LEDs) and others use liquid crystal shutters (LCSs). Essentially, they do the same thing that a laser beam does, but there are some differences. The laser beam is a single beam that is swept across the drum by a complex system of rotating mirrors. The LED system has a single row of tiny LEDs at a density of 300 per inch. The LCS system has a strip, or tiny wall, of liquid crystal substance near the drum. Behind the liquid crystal substance is a halogen light. The individual pixels in the liquid crystal can be turned on electronically to let light shine through and sensitize the drum or can be left off to block the light. The end result from a laser, LED, or LCS machine is about the same, but more companies use the laser engine and it has become the standard.

Engine

The drum and its associated mechanical attachments are called the engine. Canon is one of the foremost makers of engines. They manufacture them for their own laser printers and copy machines and for dozens of other companies such as Hewlett-Packard and Apple. There are several other Japanese companies that manufacture laser engines.

The Hewlett-Packard LaserJet was one of the first low-cost lasers. It was a fantastic success and became the de facto standard. There are now hundreds of laser printers on the market. Most of them emulate the LaserJet standard. Hewlett-Packard has become the IBM of the laser world. Almost all of the laser printers emulate the HP Laser-Jet series. Even IBM's laser printer emulates the Hewlett-Packard.

Low-cost laser printers

Competition among printer manufacturers has been a great benefit to consumers, driving prices down and forcing many new improvements. Several new low-cost models have been introduced that print 8 to 10 pages per minute instead of the 4 to 6 pages of the original models. They are smaller than the originals and can easily sit a desktop. Most have 512K of memory with an option to add more. The discount price for some of these models is now down to less than $700. The original 8-PPM HP LaserJet model has dropped from about $3500 to around $1500. If you can afford to wait a few seconds, the 4 to 6 page models will do almost everything the 8 to 10 pages will do. The prices will drop even more as the competition increases and the economies of scale in the manufacturing process become greater.

A recent ad in the *Computer Shopper* offered a Panasonic KX-P4420 laser for $779. It can print 8 pages per minute, and comes with 22 fonts, 512K memory, and several other goodies. The HP LaserJet III has about the same features as this printer. The LaserJet III was advertised for $1459 in the same issue of the *Computer Shopper*, about twice the cost of the Panasonic. The HP Laserjet IIP, a 4-PPM printer was advertised for $979.

For doing graphics, *PC Magazine* reported that the inexpensive 4-PPM units could print a page of graphics at about the same speed as the 8-PPM units. If you need a laser primarily for graphics, you can save quite a lot of money if you buy a 4-PPM unit.

Extras for lasers

Don't be surprised if you go into a store to buy a laser printer that was advertised for $1000 and end up paying a lot more. The laser printer business is more like the automobile business. I have seen laser printers advertised in the Los Angeles area for a very low price. But somewhere in the ad, in very small print, they say, "w/o toner cartridge and cables." They might charge up to $150 for the toner cartridge and up to $50 for a $5 cable. Extra fonts, memory, special controller boards, and software cost extra. Some printers have small bin feeders. A large one might cost $200 or more.

Memory

If you plan to do any graphics or desktop publishing, you will need to have at least 1Mb of memory in your machine. Of course, the more memory, the better. Laser memory chips are usually in SIMM packages. Not all lasers use the same configuration, so check before you buy. Several companies offer laser memories, including:

- ASP (800) 445-6190
- Elite (800) 942-0018

Page-description languages

If you plan to do any complex desktop publishing you might need a page-description language (PDL). Text characters and graphic images are two different species of animal. Monitor controller boards usually have all of the alphabetic and numeric characters stored in ROM. When you press the letter A on the keyboard, it dives into the ROM chip, drags out the A, and displays it in a precise block of pixels wherever the cursor happens to be. These are called bit-mapped characters. If you want to display an A that is twice as large, you have to have a complete font set of that type in the computer.

Printers are very much like monitors and have the same limitations. They have a library of stored discrete characters for each font that they can print. My Star dot matrix printer has an internal font and two cartridge slots. Several different font cartridges can be plugged into these slots, but it is limited to those fonts that happen to be plugged in.

With a good PDL, a printer can take one of the stored fonts and change it or scale it to any size you want. These are *scalable fonts*. With a bit-mapped font, you have one type face and one size. With scalable fonts, you have one typeface with an infinite number of sizes. Most of the laser printers will accept ROM cartridges that have 35 or more fonts. You can print almost anything you want with scalable fonts, provided your system can scale them.

Laser speed

Laser printers can print from 4 to more than 10 pages per minute depending on the model and what they are printing. Some expensive high-end printers can print more than 30 pages per minute.

A dot matrix printer is concerned with a single character at a time. A laser printer composes, then prints a whole page at a time. With a PDL, many different fonts, sizes of type, and graphics can be printed. But the laser must determine where every dot that makes up a character or image is to be placed on the paper before it is printed. This composition is done in memory before the page is printed. The more complex the page, the more memory is required, and the more time it will need to compose the page. It might take several minutes to compose a complex graphic. Once composed, it prints very quickly.

The PDL controls and tells the laser where to place the dots on the sheet. Adobe's PostScript is the best known PDL. Several companies have developed their own PDLs. Of course, none of them compatible with the others. This has caused a major problem for software developers because they must try to include drivers for each one of these PDLs. Several companies are attempting to clone PostScript, but it is doubtful that they can achieve complete compatibility. Unless you need to move your files from a machine that does not have PostScript to one that does, you might not need to be compatible.

PostScript printers

Printers sold with PostScript installed, such as the Apple LaserWriter, might cost as much as $1500 more than a printer without PostScript. Hewlett-Packard is offering a PostScript option for their LaserJet IID (the IID and IIID print duplex; that is, on both sides of the paper) for $995. The PostScript option for the IIP and III printers is $695.

Pacific Data Products has a cartridge that has built-in bitstream fonts comparable to Adobe's PostScript. Several other companies are also developing PostScript clones.

PostScript on disk

Several software companies have developed PostScript software emulation. One of the better ones is LaserGo's GoScript. QMS offers UltraScript and Custom Applications has Freedom of the Press.

Resolution

Almost all lasers have a 300×300 DPI resolution, which is very good, but not nearly as good as the 1200×1200 DPI used for typeset publications.

Several companies have developed systems to increase the number of dots to 600×600 DPI or more. LaserMaster has developed printer controllers that plug into a slot in the computer. There are several models that can increase resolution from 400×400 up to 1000×1000. They are rather expensive, ranging from $2000 to almost $6000.

Technology does not stand still. At the Fall 1991 COMDEX, IBM introduced their improved line of laser printers. They have a resolution of 600×600 DPI. By the time you read this, I am sure that Hewlett-Packard and most of the other companies will also have printers that have the same or better resolution.

At 300×300 DPI, it is possible to print 90,000 dots in 1 square inch. On an 8½ inch by 11-inch sheet of paper, if you deduct a 1-inch margin from the top, the bottom, and both sides, then you would have 58.5 square inches $\times$ 90,000 dots = 5,265,000 possible dots. At 600×600 DPI, the resolution is quadrupled, or 360,000 dots in 1 square inch. It is possible to have 21,060,000 dots per page.

Maintenance

Most laser printers use a toner cartridge that is good for 3000 to 5000 pages. The original cost of the cartridge is about $100. MEI/Micro Center offers new cartridges for several models at prices of $58.97 to $73.97. Several companies will refill your spent cartridges for about $50 each, including:

- Laser's Edge Products (515) 472-7850
- Lasertek   (800) 252-7374

There are many other companies. Look for ads in the computer magazines.

Of course, there are other maintenance costs. These machines are very similar to copy machines; they have a lot of moving parts that can wear out and jam up. Most of the larger companies quote MTBF figures of 30,000 to 100,000 pages. But remember, these are only average figures and not a guarantee. Most of the lasers are expected to have an overall lifetime of about 300,000 pages.

Paper and address labels

There are many different types, weights, and sizes of paper. Almost any paper will work in your laser, but if you use a cheap grade of paper, it could leave lint inside the machine and affect print quality. Generally, any bond paper or a good paper made for copiers works fine. Colored paper made for copiers will also work.

Many laser printers are equipped with trays to print envelopes. Hewlett-Packard recommends envelopes with diagonal seams and gummed flaps. Make certain that the leading edge of the envelope has a sharp crease.

Most laser printers are limited to 8½-inch by 11-inch paper (A size). The QMS PS2200 and the Unisys AP 9230 can print on 11-inch by 17-inch paper (B size) as well as the A size.

Avery has developed address labels that can withstand the heat of the fusing mechanism in a laser printer. Most office supply stores carry these labels. Avery has also developed an excellent software program that can be used to print labels. The program has a database where addresses, phone numbers, and other information can be stored. The addresses can be searched, sorted, edited, or printed. The program can also read and import data and files from dBASE and WordPerfect. It can also import .PCX and .PCC graphics files. Avery has both laser and dot matrix versions of the program ideal for anyone who does a lot of mailing.

There are also other specialty supplies that can be used with your laser. Integraphix carries several different items that you might find useful.

Color

A few color printers are available at a cost of $5000 to $15,000. These printers are often referred to as color laser printers, but they don't actually use the laser technology. They use a variety of thermal transfer technologies using wax or rolls of plastic polymer. The wax or plastic is brought into contact with the paper and heat is applied. The melted wax or plastic material adheres to the paper. Very precise points, up to 300 DPI, can be heated. By overlaying three or four colors, all of the colors of the rainbow can be created.

The cost to print color ranges from about 5 cents a sheet to about 83 cents a sheet for the large 11-inch-by-17-inch sheets. The cost depends on the type of technology used and the manufacturer.

Most of the color printers have PostScript or they emulate PostScript. The Tektronix Phaser CP can also use the Hewlett-Packard graphics language (HPGL) to emulate a plotter. These color printers can print out a page much faster than a plotter.

Several other color printers will be on the market soon. There is lots of competition so the prices should come down.

Plotters

Plotters are devices that can draw almost any shape or design under the control of a computer. A plotter might have eight or more different colored pens. There are several different types of pens for various applications, such as writing on different types of paper or on film or transparencies. Some pens are quite similar to ball-point pens, others have a fiber-type point. The points are usually made to a very close tolerance and can be very small so that line thickness can be controlled. Line thickness can be very critical in some precise designs.

The plotter arm can be directed to choose any one of the various pens. This arm is attached to a sliding rail and is moved from one side of the paper to the other. A solenoid lowers the pen at predetermined points on the paper for it to write. While the motor is moving the arm horizontally, a second motor moves the paper vertically beneath the arm. This motor can move the paper to any predetermined point and the pen is lowered to write on that spot. The motors are controlled by predefined *X-Y* coordinates. The motors can move the pen and paper in very small increments so that almost any design can be drawn.

Plotters are ideal for such things as circuit board designs, architectural drawings, transparencies for overhead presentations, graphs, charts, and many CAD/CAM drawings. All of this can be done in as many as seven different colors.

Plotters are available in several different sizes. Some desktop units are limited to only A and B sized plots. There are other large models that can accept paper up to 4 feet wide and several feet long. A desk model might cost as little as $200 up to $2000. A large model might cost from $4000 up to $10,000. If you are doing very precise work, for instance, designing a transparency that will be photographed and used to make a circuit board, you will want one of the more accurate and more expensive machines.

Many very good graphics programs are available that can use plotters. There are several manufacturers of plotters, and again, there are no standards. Just like printers, each company has developed its own drivers. This is very frustrating for software developers who must try to include drivers in their programs for all of the various brands.

Hewlett-Packard has been one of the major plotter manufacturers. Many of the other manufacturers now emulate Hewlett-Packard drivers. Almost all of the software that requires plotters includes a driver for Hewlett-Packard. If you are in the market for a plotter, try to make sure that it can emulate Hewlett-Packard. Houston Instruments is another major manufacturer of plotters, but their plotters are somewhat less expensive than Hewlett-Packards.

One of the disadvantages of plotters is that they are rather slow. There are now some software programs that allow laser printers to act as plotters. Of course, this is much faster than a plotter, but except for the colored printers, they are limited to black and white.

Plotter supplies

It is important that a good supply of plotter pens, special paper, film, and other supplies be kept on hand. Plotter supplies are not as widely available as printer supplies. Most of the plotter vendors provide supplies for their equipment. One company that specializes in plotter pens, plotter media, accessories, and supplies is:

PLOTPRO
P.O. Box 800370
Houston, TX 77280
(800) 223-7568

Installing a printer or plotter

Most IBM compatible computers allow for four ports—two serial and two parallel. No matter whether it is a plotter, dot matrix, daisywheel, or laser printer, it will require one of these ports. These ports might be built into the motherboard. If you have built-in ports, you will still need a short cable from the motherboard to the outside. You will then need a longer cable to your printer. If you don't have built-in ports, you will have to buy interface boards.

Almost all laser and dot matrix printers use the parallel ports. Some of them have both serial and parallel ports. Many of the daisywheel printers and most of the plotters use serial ports. For the serial printers, you will need a board with an RS-232C connector. The parallel printers use a Centronics-type connector. When you buy a printer, buy a cable from the vendor that is configured for your printer and your computer.

Printer sharing

Ordinarily, a printer sits idle most of the time. There are some days when I don't even turn my printer on. Most large offices and businesses have several computers, and almost all of them are connected to a printer in some fashion.

It is fairly simple to arrange it so that a printer or plotter can be used by several computers. If there are only two or three computers, and they are fairly close together, it is not much of a problem. Manual switch boxes are available, ranging in cost from $25 to $150, that allow any one of two or three computers to be switched on-line to a printer.

Switch boxes cannot be used if the computers use the parallel ports or are more than 10 feet away from the printer. Parallel signals begin to degrade if the cable is longer than 10 feet. A serial cable can be as long as 50 feet.

If an office or business is fairly complex, then several electronic switching devices are available. Some of them are very sophisticated and allow a large number of different types of computers to be attached to a single printer or plotter. Many of them have built-in buffers and allow cable lengths up to 500 feet or more. The costs range from $160 to $1400.

Networks are available that connect computers and printers together. Some of them can be rather expensive. One of the least expensive methods of sharing a printer is for a person to generate the text to be printed out on one computer, record it on a floppy diskette, and walk over to a computer that is connected to a printer. If it is in a large office, a single, low-cost XT clone could be dedicated to a high-priced printer. There are just too many laser and plotter companies to list them all. Look for ads in your local paper and in any computer magazine.

Chapter 13

Using your computer in business

Very few businesses exist that cannot benefit from the use of a computer including real estate offices, insurance brokers, travel agencies, video rental stores, doctors, dentists, architects, design engineers, retail stores, garages and service stations, machine shops, manufacturing shops, restaurants, furniture stores, print shops, hobby and craft stores, clothing stores, car sales, car rentals, beauty salons, CPAs and tax preparers, bookkeeping services, photo processors, motels, bars, physical fitness salons, nurseries, contractors, repair services, day-care centers, nursing homes, and almost any other kind of business, trade, or service.

Home office

Many businesses can be operated from a home office. Several advantages in having a home office are no commuting, no high office rent, possibly no need for day care for young children, setting your own hours, and many other advantages.

There are some disadvantages to working at home. If your partner works away from home and you are home all day, he or she might expect you to do all of the housework, shopping, cooking, and other household chores. Another disadvantage is that it might be hazardous to your health. When I am writing and get stuck, I raid the refrigerator, I gain several unneeded pounds every time I write a book.

Deducting the cost of your computer

If you have a home office, you might be able to deduct part of the cost of your computer from your income tax. You might even be able to deduct a portion of your rent, telephone bills, and other legitimate business expenses.

Some IRS rules

I can't give you all of the IRS rules for a home office, but the book, *J.K. Lasser's Your Income Tax* has a few details. This book says that

> You may operate your business from your home, using a room or other space as an office or area to assemble or prepare items for sale. To deduct home office expenses allocated to this activity, as a self-employed person, you must be able to prove that you use the home area exclusively and on a regular basis either as:
>
> A place of business to meet or deal with patients, clients, or customers in the normal course of your business. . ..
>
> Your principal place of business . . . where you spend most of your working time and most of your business income is attributable to your activities there . . ..
>
> Exclusive use and regular basis tests. If you use a room, such as a den, both for business and family purposes, you must be prepared to show that a specific section of the den is used exclusively as office space. A partition or other physical separation of the office area is helpful but not required . . . .
>
> Depending on your income . . . a deduction for home business use may include real estate taxes, mortgage interest, operating expenses (such as home in-

surance premiums and utility costs), and depreciation allocated to the area used for business . . . a pro rata share of the cost of painting the outside of a house or repairing a roof may be deductible . . ..

I can't list all of the rules and regulations, so before you deduct anything, I recommend that you buy the latest tax books and consult with the IRS or a tax expert. There are many, many rules and regulations, and they change frequently. For more information, call the IRS and ask for publication #587, *Business Use of Your Home*. Look in your telephone directory for the local or 800 number for the IRS.

Tax preparation

Congress and the IRS change the tax laws every year. The laws become more and more complex and very complicated every year making it harder for the average person to prepare their own taxes. The CPAs, tax lawyers, and tax preparers have guaranteed job security. If you are looking for a good, well-paying profession, you might consider tax preparation. This is a business that can be operated out of a home or small office.

Several software companies offer tax programs. I list some of them in the next chapter.

Retail sales

Most retail outlets and stores use a cash register. There are several types of cash registers that will work with a computer. This can help keep track of sales, inventory, and much more.

Point of sale

Point of sale (POS) terminals are usually a combination of a cash drawer, a computer, and special software. They provide fast customer checkout, credit card handling, audit and security, accounting, and reduce paperwork. By keying in the codes for various items, the computer can keep a running inventory of everything that is sold. The store owner immediately knows when to reorder certain goods. A POS system can provide instant sales analysis data as to which items sell best, buying trends, and of course, the cost and the profit or loss.

There are several different POS systems. A simple cash drawer with a built-in 40-column receipt printer might cost as little as $500. More complex systems might cost $1500 and more. Software might cost from $17 to $1000. In most successful businesses that sell goods, a POS system can easily pay for itself. They can also replace your bookkeeper and accountant. Figure 13-1 shows a POS system. If the business has more than one cash register, it is possible to tie them together in a simple network.

A few of the POS hardware and software companies include:

- Alpha Data Systems   (404) 499-9247
- Computer Time   (800) 456-1159

13-1 A POS system.

- Datacap Systems   (215) 699-7051
- Kimtron   (408) 436-6550
- Merit Digital Systems (604) 985-1391
- NCR Corp.   (800) 544-3333
- Printer Products   (617) 254-1200
- Softpoint   (408) 253-5700
- Synchronics   (901) 761-1166

Bar codes

Bar codes are a system of black-and-white lines that are arranged in a system much like the dots and dashes of Morse code. By using combinations of wide and narrow bars and wide and narrow spaces, any numeral or letter of the alphabet can be represented.

Bar codes were first adopted by the grocery industry. A central office was set up that assigned a unique number, a universal product code (UPC), for just about every manufactured and prepackaged product sold in grocery stores. Different sizes of the same product have a different and unique number assigned to them. The same type products from different manufacturers also have unique numbers.

When the clerk runs an item across the scanner, the dark bars absorb light and the white bars reflect light. The scanner decodes this number and sends it to the main computer. The computer then matches the input number to the number stored on its hard disk. Linked to the number on the hard disk is the price of the item, the description, the amount in inventory, and several other pieces of information about the item. The computer sends back the price and the description of the item to the cash register where it is printed out. The computer then deducts that item from the overall inventory and adds the price to the overall cash received for the day.

A store might have several thousand items with different sizes and prices. Without a bar-code system the clerk must know most of the prices and enter them in the cash register by hand. Many errors are committed. With bar codes, the human factor is eliminated. The transactions are performed much faster and with almost total accuracy.

At the end of the day, the manager can look at the computer output and immediately know such things as how much business was done, what inventories need to be replenished, and what items were the biggest sellers. With the push of a button, he or she can change any or all of the prices in the store.

Bar codes can be used to increase productivity, to keep track of time charged to a particular job, and to track inventory. Very few businesses, large or small, would not benefit from the use of bar codes.

There are several different types of bar-code readers or scanners. Some are actually small portable computers that can store data, which is then downloaded into a larger computer. Some systems require their own interface card that must be plugged into one of the slots on the computer motherboard. Some companies have devised systems that can be inserted in series with the keyboard so that no slot or other interface is needed. Key Tronic has a keyboard with a bar-code reader as an integral part of the keyboard.

Whole books have been written about the bar code and other means of identification. Hundreds of vendors and companies offer services in this area. If you are interested in the bar code and automatic identification technology, there are two magazines that are sent free to qualified subscribers:

- *ID Systems*, 174 Concord Street, Peterborough, NH 03458
- *Automatic I.D. News*, P.O. Box 6158, Duluth, MN 55806-9858

Write for subscription qualification forms. Almost everyone who has a business can qualify.

Local area networks

If you have a small business where there are several other computers, you might consider connecting them together into a local area network (LAN). A LAN allows accessing and sharing by all connected terminals of databases, files, information, and software. A LAN allows multitasking, multiusers, security, centralized backup, and shared resources such as printers, modems, fax machines, and other peripherals.

A network system might consist of only two computers tied together or as many as 100 or more terminals or stations. The terminals can be inexpensive XTs, or a combination of PCs, 286s, 386s, or 486s. Some network systems even allow the mixing of DOS, Macintosh, and Unix systems.

Of course, the larger the network and the more complex it is, the more expensive it will be. If you have a small business you might not need a large network or one that is very sophisticated. There are many types of LANs with many levels of complexity.

Low-cost switches and LANs

You might have just a couple of computers and you want them to share a printer or switch from a laser printer to a dot matrix. This can be done very easily with mechanical switch boxes. Some switch boxes can handle the switching needs of as many as four or five systems. These boxes can cost from $50 to more than $500. There are many vendors. Look through any of the computer magazines. Several companies provide low-cost LANs that use the RS-232 serial port, including:

- Applied Knowledge   (408) 739-3000
- DeskLink   (800) 662-2652
- LanLink 5X   (800) 766-5465
- LANtastic   (602) 293-6363
- Moses Computers   (408) 358-1550

LAN magazines

Most computer magazines occasionally carry articles on networking. However, several computer magazines are entirely dedicated to networking and are sent free to qualified subscribers:

- Novell *LAN Times*, 151 East 1700 So, Suite 100, Provo, UT 84606
- CMP *Network Computing*, 600 Community Dr., Manhasset, NY 11030

Write for subscription qualification forms.

Books on LAN

Several books have been published on networking. If you have a small business with several computers, you might want to order my book, *Build Your Own Local Area Network And Save A Bundle*, published by TAB/McGraw-Hill. Other titles from TAB/McGraw-Hill include

- *TOPS: The IBM/Macintosh Connection*, S. Cobb and M. Jost, No. 3210
- *Networking with the IBM Token-Ring*, C. Townsend, No. 2829
- *Networking with Novell NetWare, A LAN Manager's Handbook*, Paul Christiansen, Steve King, and Mark Munger, No. 3283
- *Networking with 3 + Open*, Stan Schatt, No. 3437

You can order these from TAB Books, Blue Ridge Summit, PA 17294-0850 or call (800) 822-8138. Ask for a current catalog.

Desktop publishing

Desktop publishing covers a lot of territory. A simple system might consist of an XT with a word processor and a dot matrix printer. A large system might include laser printers, PostScript, scanners, 386 or 486 computers with many megabytes of hard disk space, and sophisticated software. As always, the type of system you need depends on what you want it to do (and of course, how much money you want to spend). Desktop publishing can be used for newsletters, ads, flyers, brochures, sales proposals, sophisticated manuals, and all sorts of printed documents.

Desktop publishing software

If your project isn't too complex, you can probably do a good job with a laser printer and a word processing program such as WordStar for Windows, WordPerfect for Windows, Word for Windows, AMI, and several others. If you are doing a more complicated and professional type of DTP, with a lot of graphics and different types and fonts, then you might need one of the higher-level software packages. The premier high-end packages are Ventura from Xerox and PageMaker from Aldus. GEM Desktop Publisher from DRI and InteGraphics from IMSI are much less expensive and will do almost everything you need to do for a lot less money. There are many, many other software packages ranging from $89 to $15,000. A few companies that supply page layout software include

Company	Product	Phone
Acorn Plus	Easy Laser	(213) 876-5237
Aldus	PageMaker	(206) 622-5500
Ashton-Tate	Byline	(800) 437-4327
CSI Publishing	Pagebuilder	(800) 842-2486
Data Transforms	Fontrix	(303) 832-1501
Digital Research	GEM DTP	(800) 443-4200
Haba/Arrays	Front Page	(818) 994-1899
IMSI	InteGraphics	(415) 454-8901
LTI Softfonts	Laser-Set	(714) 739-1453
Savtek	ETG Plus	(800) 548-7173
Timeworks	Publish It	(800) 535-9497
Xerox	Ventura	(800) 832-6979

Clip art

Several software packages are available with images that you can import and place in your page layout. The software lets you move the images around, rotate, size, or revise them. The images include humans, animals, business, technical, industrial, borders, enhancements, etc. Most of the companies have the images set up in modules on floppies. And most have several modules with hundreds and even thousands of images.

A few companies that supply clip art include

Company	Product	Phone
Antic	Cyber Design	(800) 234-7001
Artware Systems	Artware	(800) 426-3858
CD Designs	Graphics	(800) 326-5326
EMS Shareware	DTP Library	(301) 924-3594

Company	Product	Phone
Kinetic Corp.	U.S. Maps	(502) 583-1679
Metro ImageBase	Picture Pak	(800) 525-1552
Micrografx	Charisma	(800) 272-3729
PCsoftware	Exec. Picture	(619) 571-0981
Springboard	Clip Art	(800) 445-4780
Studio Ad Art	Click & Clip	(800) 453-1860

Books for DTP

TAB/McGraw-Hill publishes several books on the subject of desktop publishing, including:

Mastering PageMaker, G. Keith Gurganus, No. 3176
Ventura Publisher, Elizabeth McClure, No. 3012
The Print Shop Companion, P. Seyer and H. Leitch, No. 3218
IBM Desktop Publishing, G. Lanyi and J. Barrett, No. 3109
Desktop Publishing & Typesetting, M.L. Kleper, No. 2700

You can order these book from TAB Books, Blue Ridge Summit, PA 17294-0850 or call (800) 822-8138.

DTP Magazines

There are several magazines that are devoted to desktop publishing including:

Publish, P.O. Box 51966, Boulder, CO 80321-1966
PC Publishing, P.O. Box 5050, Des Plaines, IL 60017
EP&P, 650 S. Clark St., Chicago, IL 60605-9960

PC Publishing and *EP&P* are free if you qualify. Most other magazines listed in chapter 15 often have DTP articles.

Chapter 14

Essential software

You will probably never have to do any programming. There is more software already written and immediately available, than you can use in a lifetime. Except for very unusual applications, the ordinary user should never have to do any programming. There are off-the-shelf programs that can do almost everything that you could ever want to do with a computer.

Off-the-shelf and ready-to-use software

For most general applications, there are certain basic programs that you will need. Speaking of basic, BASIC is one that is needed. GW-BASIC from Microsoft is more or less the standard. GW-BASIC is included with all versions of DOS. Many applications still use BASIC. Even if you are not a programmer, it is simple enough that anyone can design a few special applications with it.

You will need several categories of programs such as a disk operating system (DOS), word processors, databases, spreadsheets, utilities, shells, communications, Windows, graphics, and computer-aided design (CAD). Depending on what you intend to use your computer for, there are hundreds of others for special needs.

Software can be more expensive than hardware. It will pay to shop around. I have seen software with a list price of $700 advertised by a discount house for as little as $350. Also, remember that there are excellent public domain programs that can do almost everything that high-cost commercial programs can do, and they are free. Check your local bulletin board, user group, or the ads for public domain software in most computer magazines. There are also some excellent shareware programs that can be registered for a very nominal sum.

I can't possibly list all of the thousands of software packages available. Again, subscribe to the magazines listed in chapter 15. Most of them have detailed reviews of software in every issue. I will briefly discuss some of the essential software packages that you will need in the following sections.

Operating systems software

DOS to a computer is like gasoline to an automobile. Without it, it won't operate. DOS is an acronym for disk operating system, but it does much more than just operate the disks. In recognition of this, the new OS/2 has dropped the D.

If you are new to computers, DOS should be the first thing you learn. DOS has more than 50 commands, but chances are you will never need to know more than 15 or 20 of them.

MS-DOS

You can use any version of DOS on your computer. I don't know why anyone would want to, but you can even use version 1.0. Of course, you would be severely limited in what you could do. I recommend that you buy MS-DOS 5.0 or DR-DOS 6.0.

When the operating system, config.sys, buffers, drivers, TSRs, and other files are loaded into the 640K of available RAM, there is often not enough memory left to load other programs. DR-DOS 6.0 and MS-DOS 5.0 take the operating system, TSRs, buffers, and drivers out of low memory and place them in memory above 640K. The older versions of DOS loaded everything into low memory. Quite often there was not enough RAM left over to run many programs.

There are many good commands in DOS, and there are some that if not used properly, can be disastrous. Be very careful when using commands such as FOR-MAT, DEL, ERASE, COPY, and RECOVER. When invoked, RECOVER renames and turns all of the files into FILE0001.REC, FILE0002.REC . . ..The disk will no longer be bootable and critical files might be garbled. Many experts say that you should erase the RECOVER command from your disk files and leave it only on your original diskettes. It should only be used as a last resort. Norton Utilities, Mace Utilities, PC Tools, or one of the other utility softwares is much better for unerasing or restoring a damaged file.

Copy can cause problems if you copy a file onto a disk that has another file with the same name. The file with the same name will be replaced and gone forever. If you erase or delete a file, you can possibly recover it. But if it has been copied over or written over, it is history.

DR-DOS 6.0

The DR is in DOS 6.0 for *Digital Research*, not doctor. The Digital Research Corporation was founded by Gary Kidahl, the devel óper of CP/M, the first operating system for personal computers. DR-DOS 6.0 is completely compatible with MS-DOS. DR-DOS 6.0 has several good features. One is FileLINK, which allows you to connect and transfer files through a serial cable. It also has ViewMAX to view, organize, and execute files and commands using only one or two keystrokes or a mouse. It has comprehensive on-line help, supports hard disk partitions up to 512Mb, has disk cache, a full-screen text editor, password protection, and many features not found in MS-DOS.

If you work in a large office you might want to keep some of your nosy neighbors from snooping into your personal files. DR-DOS 6.0 allows you to use a password to protect your files.

The ViewMAX shell feature allows DR-DOS to use icons to operate, much like Windows 3.0. You can use a mouse to quickly open files, copy, delete, and perform many of the other commands and functions. ViewMAX also has a clock that can run in a window of the screen. Another feature is a calculator for on-screen calculations.

DR-DOS is very easy to install on a hard disk, just copy it onto the disk. There is no need to reformat your disk. If you have a previous version of DOS on your disk, it will copy over and replace the older DOS. It has the same commands and is fully compatible with DOS. DR-DOS is now part of the Novell Company.

OS/2

OS/2 2.0 was introduced at the Spring COMDEX in April of 1992. It comes complete with MS-DOS 5.0 and Windows 3.0. (They promised to update to Windows 3.1 shortly.) OS/2 also has Adobe Type Manager (ATM) that allows scalable fonts for Windows and for printing. It has several other excellent utilities and goodies.

OS/2 2.0 breaks the 640K barrier and can seamlessly address more than 4 gigabytes of RAM. It can do true multitasking and run several programs at the same time.

If one program crashes, it does not affect the other programs. It can run all DOS software and any of the software that has been developed for Windows. There are even a few games such as solitaire and chess if you have nothing else to do.

IBM claims that OS/2 runs Windows applications under MS-DOS better than Windows. Many people bought Macintosh computers because they are easy to use and learn. IBM's OS/2 has many similarities with the Macintosh. For some applications, it might even be easier to use than the Macintosh. Apple is not complaining, however, because IBM is now a partner.

Currently, not much software can take advantage of its 32-bit capabilities. But at the Spring COMDEX introduction, more than 800 companies pledged to develop 32-bit software for OS/2.

One disadvantage of OS/2 is that it requires more than 25Mb of hard disk space and about 6Mb of RAM. The good news is that hard disks and memory prices are dropping everyday. The advantages of its vast capabilities far outweigh the disadvantages of being a memory hog.

Another great advantage is that it is very inexpensive. IBM gave away thousands of copies at COMDEX. They are also pricing it from $49 up to $149. For this price, you get MS-DOS 5.0, Windows 3.0, Adobe Type Manager, and many other utilities. My copy came on 21 1.44Mb floppy disks. The 21 disks alone, even if they were blank, would be worth $49.

Windows 3.1

Windows 3.0 was one of the most phenomenal successes of all time, but it had some flaws. Microsoft has extensively revised 3.1 and added several new features. One added option is TrueType scalable fonts for the screen and for printing. This can give you true what-you-see-is-what-you-get (WYSIWYG). They also added an extensive list of printer drivers that can print faster and has a better SMARTDrive, with read and write caching.

One flaw in 3.0 was that it often caused the computer to hang up with unrecoverable application errors (UAE). The whole system would then have to be rebooted. If you had work that was not saved to disk or you had two or more windows open, everything was lost.

The new Windows 3.1 does away with UAEs. If there is an error, the program analyzes it and gives you several options. Dr. Watson, a diagnostic utility asks you to describe the details of what happened. These comments are saved as a record and used to help Microsoft or other developers eliminate problems. If the program does crash, only that operation goes down. Other open windows are not affected.

Microsoft also added an object linking and embedding (OLE) utility to allow data or graphics in one file to be imported and embedded in another. They have also built in sound capabilities with sound boards such as Sound Blaster (408) 986-1461, Pro AudioSpectrum (800) 638-2807, Soundcards (213) 685-5141, and Multisound (717) 843-6916.

Windows NT

There are other improvements in Windows 3.1, but it is still a 16-bit system. At this moment, Microsoft is working overtime to complete Windows NT (new technology) a 32-bit system to complete head-to-head with OS2 2.0. The outcome will be interesting and quite beneficial to us, the consumer.

New Wave 4.0

Hewlett-Packard's New Wave adds several important features that makes Windows 3.1 even better. It lets you use more than 11 characters to name a file and lets you create objects, put them in folders, and manage them. You can use New Wave to create multiple views of objects and create Macros to automate tasks. It also has several other good utilities not found in Windows 3.1. New Wave is an essential adjunct to 3.1.

Norton desktop for Windows 2.0

The Norton DTP for Windows has all of the utilities found in Norton's Utilities for DOS plus several others. It also includes the Norton's Backup. It, too, is an essential adjunct to 3.1.

DESQview

DESQview, from Quarterdeck Office Systems, is similar to Windows in some respects in that it runs on top of DOS, and it allows multitasking and multiusers. You can have up to 50 programs running at the same time and have as many as 250 windows open. It runs all DOS software. It is simple to learn and use. Early versions of DESQview caused a conflict in memory when run under Windows 3.0. New versions now run under Windows 3.0 with no problems.

DOS help programs

Learning DOS can be very difficult and several help programs have been developed. One such program is Doctor DOS from VMG. The Phoenix Company, one of the first developers of a clone BIOS, also has an excellent help program for learning DOS. There are many others, even some public domain programs. Look for ads in computer magazines. I have included a disk with this book that can help you.

Word processors

The most-used software of all is word processing. There are literally hundreds of word processor packages, each one slightly different than the others. It amazes me that they can find so many different ways to do the same thing. Most word processing programs come with a spelling checker, and some of them come with a thesaurus. They might also include several other utilities for such things as communications programs for your modem, outlines, desktop publishing, print merging, and many others. There are many other good word processors than those listed in this section. Look through computer magazines for reviews.

WordStar

I started off with WordStar on my little CP/M Morrow with a hefty 64K of memory and two 140K single-sided disk drives. It took me some time to learn it. I have tried several other word processors since then and found that most of them would require almost as much time to learn as WordStar did originally.

There are probably more copies of WordStar in existence than any other word processor. Most magazine and book editors expect their writers to send manuscripts to them on a diskette in WordStar. Newer versions work under Windows.

WordStar has an educational division that offers an excellent discount to schools, both for site licenses and for student purchases. You can contact the educational division by calling (800) 543-8188.

WordPerfect

WordPerfect is one of the hottest-selling word processors so it must be doing something right. One thing they are doing right is giving free, unlimited support. WordPerfect has the ability to select fonts by a proper name. It has simplified printer installation and the ability to do most desktop publishing functions, columns, and many other useful functions and utilities. It also works with Windows.

Microsoft Word for Windows

Microsoft Word for Windows was developed by the same people who gave us MS-DOS. It lets you take advantage of all the features and utilities of Windows. It is among the best-sellers in the country. If you already know a different word processor, Word for Windows includes a manual that lists the differences in most of the popular word processors. It can help you quickly become accustomed to Word for Windows.

PC-Write

PC-Write, from QuickSoft, is the least expensive of the word processors. It is shareware and is free if copied from an existing user. They ask for a $16 donation. Full registration with manual and technical support is $89. PC-Write is easy to learn and is an excellent personal word processor. QuickSoft (800) 888-8088.

Grammar checkers

You might be the most intelligent person alive, but you might not be able to write a simple intelligible sentence. There are several grammar checking programs, including Right Writer, by Que Corp., and Grammatik by Reference Software, that work with most of the word processors. These programs analyze your writing and suggest ways to improve it.

Database programs

Database programs are very useful for managing large amounts of information by allowing you to store it, search it, sort it, do calculations, make up reports, and other useful features.

Currently, there are almost as many database programs as there are word processors. Few of them are compatible with each other. There is a strong effort in the industry to establish some standards under the structured query language (SQL). Several of the larger companies have announced their support for this standard.

dBASE IV

Ashton-Tate's dBASE II was one of the first companies that offered a database program for the personal computer. It is a very powerful program and has hundreds of features, but it is a highly structured program and can be a bit difficult to learn. dBASE IV is much faster than dBASE III, has a built-in compiler, SQL, and an upgraded user interface along with several other enhancements. Ashton-Tate is now a division of Borland.

askSam

This funny looking name—askSam—is an acronym for access knowledge via stored access method. It is a free-form, text-oriented database management system from Seaside Software. It is almost like a word processor. Data can be typed in randomly, then sorted and accessed. Data can also be entered in a structured format for greater organization. It is not quite as powerful as dBASE IV, but is much easier to use. It is also much less expensive and is ideal for personal use and for the majority of business needs.

Students can buy the $295 program for only $45 when the order is placed by an instructor. Any instructor who places an order for 10 or more copies will get a free copy. This is a fantastic bargain.

R:BASE 3.1

R:BASE has been around for a long time. It was recently revised and updated with pull-down menus, mouse support, fully relational multi-table capability tasks, and an English-like procedural language. It is one of the more powerful and more versatile of the present-day database programs. Microrim is so sure that you will like the program that they offer an unlimited, no-questions-asked, 90-day, money-back guarantee.

FoxPro

FoxPro, from Fox Software, is very easy to use. It has windows and can be controlled by a mouse or the keyboard. Of course, using it with a mouse saves several keystrokes. It has several different windows. The view window is the master control panel to create databases, open files, browse, set options, and other functions. You don't have to be a programmer to type commands into the command window. The browse window lets you view, edit, append, or delete files. It also has memo fields, a built-in editor that allows you to create macros, has extensive context-sensitive help, and much more.

Paradox

Paradox is fairly easy to learn and use and is fast and powerful. It is designed for both beginners and expert users. It is a full-featured relational database that can be used on a single PC or on a network. The main menu has functions like view, ask, report, create, modify, image, forms, tools, scripts, and help. Choosing one of these functions will bring up options that are associated with that item. Extensive use is made of the function keys.

The query by example is very helpful for beginners and experts alike. Paradox has a very powerful programming language, PAL. Experienced programmers can easily design special applications.

Paradox is one of the Borland family of products. Philippe Kahn is the founder and president of Borland. He was penniless when he came to this country from Belgium. His first product was Sidekick, then Turbo Pascal, and dozens of other products. His company has recently acquired Ashton-Tate and dBASE IV.

Spreadsheets

Spreadsheets are primarily number crunchers. In business, spreadsheets are essential for inventory, expenses, accounting purposes, forecasting, and dozens of other vital business uses. Spreadsheets have a matrix of cells in which data is entered. Data in a particular cell can be acted on by formulas and mathematical equations. If the data in the cell that is acted on affects other cells, recalculations are done on them. Several tax software programs use a simple spreadsheet. Your income and deductions are entered and if an additional deduction is discovered, it can be entered and all the calculations are done over automatically. Here are just a few of the most popular spreadsheets:

Lotus 1-2-3   Lotus was one of the first and most popular spreadsheets. It is now available in a Windows version.

Microsoft Excel   Excel is a very powerful spreadsheet program with pull-down menus, windows, and dozens of features. It can even perform as a database.

Quattro   Another Borland product, the Quattro spreadsheet looks very much like Lotus 1-2-3, but it has better graphics capabilities for charts, calculates faster, has pull-down menus, can print sideways, and has several other features not found in Lotus 1-2-3. One of the better features is the suggested list price of $195; only $148 from a discount house.

SuperCalc5   SuperCalc, introduced in 1981, was one of the pioneer spreadsheets. It has never enjoyed the popularity of Lotus, though it has features not found in Lotus. It is compatible with Lotus 1-2-3 files and can link to dBASE and several other files. It is an excellent spreadsheet. Computer Associates has also developed several excellent accounting packages costing from $595 to $695.

Utilities

Utilities are essential tools that can unerase a file, detect bad sectors on a hard disk, diagnose, unfragment, sort, and do many other things. Norton Utilities was the first, and is still foremost, in the utility department. Mace Utilities has several functions not found in Norton. Mace Gold is an integrated package of utilities that includes POP (a power out protection program), a backup utility, TextFix, and dbFix for data retrieval. PC Tools has even more utilities than Norton or Mace.

Ontrack, the people who have sold several million copies of Disk Manager for hard disks, also has a utility program called DOSUTILS. It provides tools to display and modify any physical sector of a hard disk, to scan for bad sectors, and to diagnose and analyze the disk.

Steve Gibson's SpinRite, Prime Solution's Disk Technician, and Gazelle's OP-Tune are excellent hard disk tools for low-level formatting, defragmenting, and detecting potential bad sectors on a hard disk.

Norton Utilities A program that everybody should have. Norton also has Norton Commander, a shell program, and Norton Backup, a very good hard disk backup program. Norton has recently merged with Symantec.

Mace Utilities Mace Utilities was developed by Paul Mace. Mace was recently acquired by Fifth Generation Systems, the people who developed FastBack, the leading backup program.

PC Tools PC Tools, from Central Point Software, is an excellent program that just about does it all. It has data recovery utilities, hard disk backup, a DOS shell, a disk manager, and more.

SpinRite II SpinRite, from Gibson Research, can check the interleave and reset it for the optimum factor and can do it without destroying your data. It can also test a hard drive and detect any marginal areas. SpinRite can maximize hard disk performance and prevent hard disk problems before they happen. Steve Gibson, the developer of SpinRite, writes a very interesting weekly column for *InfoWorld*.

Disk Technician Disk Technician, from Prime Solutions, does essentially the same thing that SpinRite does, and a bit more. It has several automatic features and can now detect most viruses.

OPTune OPTune is another utility that can maximize hard disk performance. It is similar to SpinRite and Disk Technician. Gazelle Systems has also developed QDOS 3, an excellent shell program, and Back-It 4, a very good hard disk backup program.

CheckIt CheckIt, from TouchStone Software, quickly checks and reports on your computer's configuration, the type of CPU it has, the amount of memory, and the installed drives and peripherals. It runs diagnostic tests of the installed items and can do performance benchmark tests.

SideKick Plus SideKick, from Borland, is in a class by itself. It was first released in 1984 and has been the most popular pop-up program since. It has recently been revised and enlarged so that it does much more than the simple calculator, notepad, calendar, and other utilities it had originally. It now has all of the original utilities plus scientific, programmer, and business calculators, an automatic phone dialer, a sophisticated script language, and much more. SideKick loads into memory and pop ups whenever you need it, no matter what program you happen to be running at the time.

Directory and disk management programs

There are dozens of disk management programs that help you keep track of files and data, providing such features as find, rename, view, sort, copy, delete, and many other useful utilities. Directory and disk-management programs can save an enormous amount of time and make life a lot simpler.

XTreePro Gold

Executive Systems XTree was one of the first and is still one of the best disk management programs. It has recently been revised and is now much faster and has several new features.

Q DOS III

This disk management program from Gazelle Systems is similar to XTree. It does not have quite as many features as XTree, but it is less expensive.

Tree86 3.0

This low-cost disk management program from Aldridge is similar to XTree.

Wonder Plus 3.08

Wonder, or 1DIR, from Bourbaki, was one of the early disk management shells. It has recently been revised and updated.

Search utilities

I have about 3000 files on my hard disk in several subdirectories. You can imagine how difficult it is to keep track of all of them. I sometimes forget in which subdirectory I filed something. Several programs are available that can go through all of my directories and look for a file by name.

Because only eight characters can be used for a file name, it is difficult to remember what is in each file. Several programs are available that can search through your files and find almost anything that you tell it to. You don't even have to know the full name of what you are looking for. They will accept wildcards and tell you where there are matches.

Magellan 2.0

Magellan 2.0, from Lotus, is a very sophisticated program that can navigate and do global searches through files and across directories. It finds text and lets you view it in a window. It lets you compress files, do backup, compare, undelete, and several other functions.

There are several other search programs that are not quite as sophisticated as Magellan. One of them is Gofer, from Microlytics. There are also public domain and shareware search programs.

Computer-aided design (CAD)
AutoCAD

This is a high-end, high-cost design program from Autodesk. It is quite complex, with an abundance of capabilities and functions. It is also rather expensive at about $3000. There are some modules that cost less. It is the defacto standard of the CAD world for the many clones that have followed.

DesignCAD 2D and DesignCAD 3D

DesignCAD 2D and DesignCAD 3D, are from American Small Business Computers, will do just about everything that AutoCAD will do at about one-tenth of the cost. DesignCAD 3D allows you to make three-dimensional drawings. There are several other companies that offer CAD software. Check the ads in the computer magazines.

Tax programs

Because you have a computer, it might not be necessary for you to pay a tax preparer to do your taxes. There are several tax programs that can do the job you do. Unless you have a very complicated income, your taxes can be done quickly and easily. In many cases, the cost of the program is probably less than the cost of having a tax preparer do your taxes.

Besides doing your own taxes, most tax programs allow you to set up files and do the taxes of others. Of course, software vendors would like each person to buy a separate copy of the program, although many of them offer programs for professional tax businesses, they are usually more expensive.

Tax programs operate much like a spreadsheet, in that the forms, schedules, and worksheets are linked together. When you enter data at one place, other affected data is automatically updated. Some of the programs are simply templates for Lotus 1-2-3 or Symphony and require those programs to run. Most tax programs have a built-in calculator so that you can do calculations before entering figures. Many of them allow "what if" calculations to show you what your return would look like with various inputs. Some of them offer modules for state taxes for some of the larger states such as New York and California. Most of them allow you to print out IRS accepted forms.

Andrew Tobias' TaxCut

Andrew Tobias' TaxCut, from Meca Ventures, will handle most average returns. It can be interfaced with Andrew Tobias' Managing Your Money, which is an excellent personal financial program. It does not offer state modules.

J.K. Lasser's Your Income Tax

J.K. Lasser's Your Income Tax has a scratch pad, calculator, and a next-year tax planner. The popular *J.K. Lasser's Tax Guide* is included with the package.

SwifTax

SwifTax from Timeworks, has memo pads, a calculator, context-sensitive help, and allows "what ifs." It does not include state modules.

TaxView

TaxView, from SoftView, is the PC version of MacInTax, the foremost tax program for the Macintosh. It runs under Windows (a run-time version is included), and it is recommended that it be used with a mouse. It is very easy to learn and use. It has a calculator, allows "what ifs," supports a large number of IRS forms, and has California and New York state tax modules.

TurboTax

TurboTax, from ChipSoft, is unique in that it offers modules for 41 states. It has an excellent manual and is fairly easy to install and learn. It starts out with a personal interview about your financial situation for the past year. It then lists forms that you might need. Based on the present years taxes, it can estimate what your taxes will be for next year.

Miscellaneous

Programs for accounting, statistics, finance, and many other applications are also available; some are very expensive, some are very reasonable.

Money Counts

Money Counts is a very inexpensive program from Parsons Technology that can be used at home or in a small business. You can set up a budget, keep track of all of your expenses, balance your checkbook, and several other functions.

It's Legal

Another program from Parsons Technology, It's Legal, helps you create wills, leases, promissory notes, and other legal documents. Parsons Technology (800) 223-6925.

WillMaker 4.0

WillMaker 4.0 is a low-cost program from Nolo Press that can help you create a will. Everyone should have a will, no matter what age or how much you own. Many people put it off because they don't want to take the time or they don't want to pay a lawyer a large fee. This inexpensive software can help you create a legal will. Nolo Press (415) 549-1976.

The Random House Encyclopedia

Microlytics has put an entire encyclopedia on disk—the Random House Encyclopedia. This program quickly lets you find any subject. Microlytics (716) 248-9150.

ACT!

ACT!, from Contact Software, allows you to keep track of business contacts, schedules, and business expenses, write reports, and about 30 other features. Contact Software (500) 228-9228.

Form Express

Most businesses have dozens of forms that must be filled out. Usually, the information then has to be transferred to a computer. Form Express lets you design and fill in almost any type of form on a hard disk. If necessary, the forms can then be printed out. Form Express (415) 382-6600.

Summary

I can't possibly mention all of the fantastic software that is available. There are thousands and thousands of ready-made software programs that will allow you to do almost anything with your computer. Look through any computer magazine for the reviews and ads. You should be able to find programs for almost any application.

Chapter 15

Component sources

I hope that I have convinced you that you can save money by upgrading your computer yourself. How much you save will depend on what components you buy and who you buy them from. You will have to shop wisely and be fairly knowledgeable about the components in order to take advantage of good bargains.

Computer swaps

I have done almost all of my buying at computer shows and swap meets. There is at least one computer show or swap almost every weekend in larger cities. If you live in or near a large city, check your newspaper for ads. In California, there are several computer magazines, such as *MicroTimes* and *Computer Currents*, that list coming events.

One of the best features of swap meets is that almost all the components you will need are in one place on display. Several booths will have the same components. I usually take a pencil and pad with me to the shows. I walk around and write down the prices of the items that I want to buy and compare prices at various booths. There can be quite a wide variation in price. I bought a good printer at one show. One dealer was asking $995 for it in one booth, and about 50 feet away, another dealer was offering the same printer for $695.

You can also haggle with most of the dealers at these shows, especially when it gets near closing time. Rather than pack up the material and lug it back to their stores, many will sell it for a lower price.

The Interface company puts on the biggest computer shows in the country. They have a spring Computer Dealers Exposition (COMDEX) in Atlanta or Chicago and a fall COMDEX in Las Vegas, usually attracting more than 120,000 visitors for the Las Vegas show.

Support your local store

I consider myself to be fairly knowledgeable about electronics and computers. I hate to admit it, but in the past I have been sold inferior and shoddy merchandise a few times at these swaps. Most of the vendors at the swaps are local business people. They want your business and will not risk losing you as a customer. However, there might be a few vendors from other parts of the country. If you buy something from a vendor who does not have a local store, be sure to get a name and address. Most components are reliable, but there is always a chance that something might not work. You might need to exchange it or get it repaired, or you might need to ask some questions or need some support to get it working.

Again, computers are very easy to assemble. Once you have all of the components, it will take you less than an hour to assemble your computer. Most components are now fairly reliable, but still there is a possibility that a new part that you buy and install could be defective. Most dealers will give you a warranty of some kind and will replace defective parts. If there is something in the system that prevents it from operating, you might not be able to determine just which component is defective. Besides that, it can sometimes take a considerable amount of time to remove a component like a motherboard and return it to someone across town, or worse, someone across the country. So if at all possible, try to deal with a knowledgeable vendor who will support you and help you if you have any problems.

Mail order

Every computer magazine carries pages and pages of ads for compatible components and systems that you can order through the mail. If you live in an area where there are no computer stores or shows, you can buy by mail. Another reason to use mail order is because it is usually less expensive than local vendors. Most local vendors have to buy their stock from a distributor. The distributor usually buys it from the manufacturer or a wholesaler. By the time you get the product, it has passed through several companies who each have made some profit. One reason an IBM or Apple computer is more expensive is that they have several middlemen. Most of the direct marketers who advertise by mail have cut out the middlemen and pass some of their profit on to you with lower prices.

Most mail-order businesses are honest. Ads are the lifeblood of magazines. The subscription price of a magazine does not even pay the mailing costs, so they must have ads. A few bad advertisers can ruin a magazine. The magazines have formed the Microcomputer Marketing Council (MMC) of the Direct Marketing Association, 6 East 43rd St., New York, NY 10017. They have an action line at (212) 297-1393. If you have problems with a vendor that you cannot resolve, they might be able to help. They police their advertisers fairly closely.

You should be sure of what you need and what you are ordering. Some ads aren't written well and might not tell the whole story. Ads are expensive so they abbreviate or leave out a lot of important information. If possible, call first and inquire about their return policy for defective merchandise. Ask how long before the item will be shipped. Ask for the current price. Ads are usually placed about two months before the magazines are delivered or hit the stands. The way prices are coming down, there could be quite a change in cost by the time you place your order. Of course, if you send them the advertised price, I am sure they will not refuse it. A $2 or $3 phone call could save you a lot of time, trouble, and maybe even some money.

Ten rules for ordering by mail

In this section, I've put together 10 brief rules that you should follow when ordering by mail:

1. *Look for a street address.* Make sure the advertiser has a street address. In some ads, they give only a phone number. If you decide to buy from a vendor, call and verify that there is a live person on the other end with a street number. But before you send any money, do a bit more investigation. If possible, look through past issues of the same magazine for previous ads. If the vendor has been advertising for several months, then they are probably okay.

2. *Compare other vendors' prices.* Check through the magazines for other ven-

dor's prices for the product. The prices should be fairly close. If it appears to be a bargain that is too good to be true, then . . . you know the rest.

3. *Buy from MMC members.* Buy from a vendor who is a member of the Micro-computer Marketing Council of the Direct Marketing Association or other recognized association. There are about 10,000 members who belong to marketing associations who have agreed to abide by the ethical guidelines and rules of the associations. Except for friendly persuasion and the threat of expulsion, the associations have little power over their members. But most of them realize what is at stake and place a great value on their membership. Most who advertise in the major computer magazines are members.

   The U.S. Post Office, the Federal Trade Commission, the magazines, and the legitimate businessmen who advertise have taken steps to try to stop the fraud and scams.

4. *Do your homework.* Read ads carefully. Advertising space is very expensive. Many ads use abbreviations that might not be entirely clear. If in doubt, call and ask. A $2 telephone call might save you a lot of time and prevent a lot of frustration. Know exactly what you want, state precisely the model, make, size, component, and any other pertinent information. Tell them which ad you are ordering from and ask for a current price, if the item is in stock, and when you can expect delivery. If the item is not in stock, indicate whether you will accept a substitute or if you want your money refunded. Ask for an invoice or order number. Ask the person's name. Write down all of the information, the time, the date, the company's address and phone number, a description of the item, and the promised delivery date. Write down and save any information about telephone conversations including the time, the date, and the person's name. Save any and all correspondence.

5. *Ask questions.* Ask if the advertised item comes with all the necessary cables, parts, accessories, software, etc. Ask what the warranties are. Ask about the seller's return and refund policies. Ask with whom you should correspond if there is a problem.

6. *Don't send cash.* You will have no record of it. If possible, use a credit card. If you have a problem, you can possibly have the bank refuse to pay the amount. A personal check might cause a delay of three to four weeks while the vendor waits for the check to clear. A money order or credit card order should be filled and shipped immediately. Keep a copy of the money order.

7. *Ask for a delivery date.* If you have not received your order by the promised delivery date notify the seller.

8. *Try the item out as soon as you receive it.* If you have a problem, notify the seller immediately by phone, then in writing. Give all details. Don't return the merchandise unless the dealer gives you a return material authorization (RMA). Make sure to keep a copy of the shipper's receipt, packing slip, or some evidence that the material was returned.

9. *Verify that you have a problem.* If you believe a product is defective or you have a problem, reread your warranties and guarantees. Reread the manual and any documentation. It is very easy to make an error or misunderstand how an item operates if you are unfamiliar with it. Before you go to a lot of trouble, try to get some help from someone else. At least get someone to verify that you do have a problem. Many times a problem will disappear and the vendor will not be able to duplicate it. If possible, when you call, try to have the item in your computer and be at the computer so you can describe the problem as it happens.

10. *Try to work out your problem with the vendor.* If you cannot, then write to the consumer complaint agency in the seller's state. You should also write to the magazine where you saw the ad and to the DMA, 6 E. 43rd St., New York, NY 10017.

Federal Trade Commission rules

Except for sometimes having to wait for two weeks or more for delivery, I have never had any problems with mail-order vendors. You might not be so lucky. Here are six FTC rules you should know:

1. *The seller must ship within 30 days.* The seller must ship your order within 30 days unless the ad clearly states that it will take longer.

2. *Right to cancel.* If it appears that the seller cannot ship when promised, he must notify you and give you a new date. He must give you the opportunity to cancel the order and must refund your money if you desire.

3. *The seller must notify you if your order can't be filled.* If the seller notifies you that he cannot fill your order on time, he must include a stamped self-addressed envelope or card so that you can respond to his notice. If you do not respond, he can assume that you agree to the delay. He must ship within 30 days of the end of the original 30 days or cancel your order and refund your money.

4. *Right to cancel if delayed.* Even if you consent to a delay, you still have the right to cancel at any time.

5. *The seller must refund your money if your order is cancelled.* If you cancel an order that has been paid for by check or money order, the seller must refund your money. If you paid by credit card, your account must be credited within one billing cycle. Store credits or vouchers in place of a refund are not acceptable.

6. *No substitutions.* If the item you ordered is not available, the seller cannot send you a substitute without your express consent.

On-line services

If you have a modem there are several bulletin boards and on-line companies that offer all types of shopping services. You can call up from your computer and buy such things as airline tickets, furniture, clothing, toys, electronics, computers, and just about everything else you can imagine.

On-line services offer some advantages over mail order. The prices quoted in some magazines might be two or three months old by the time the magazine is published. The prices quoted by the on-line services are the latest up-to-the-minute prices. A few of the bulletin boards that offer on-line buying include:

FIRST CAPITOL COMPUTER
16 Algana
St. Peters, MO 63376
(314) 928-9889
BBS line (314) 928-9228

JDR MICRODEVICES
2233 Branham Ln.
San Jose, CA 95124
(408)559-1200
BBS line (408) 559-0253

LEO ELECTRONICS
P.O. Box 11307
Torrance, CA 95124
(213)212-6133
BBS line (213) 212-7179

SWAN TECHNOLOGIES
3075 Research Dr.
State College, PA 16801
(814) 234-2236
BBS line (814) 237-6145

Other on-line companies include:

- CompuServe   (800) 848-8990
- Delphi   (800) 544-4005
- Prodigy   (800) 776-3449
- Genie   (800) 638-9636

Sources of knowledge

Several good magazines are available that can help you gain the knowledge you need to make sensible purchases and to learn more about computers. These magazines usually carry some very interesting and informative articles and reviews of software and hardware. They also have many ads for computers, components, and software.

Some of the better magazines that you should subscribe to are *Computer Shopper*, *PC Sources*, *Byte*, *Computer Monthly*, *PC World*, and *PC Magazine*. Most of these magazines are available on local magazine racks. But you will save money with a yearly subscription and they will be delivered to your door.

If you need a source of components, you only have to look in any of the preceding magazines to find hundreds of them. If you live near a large city, there will no doubt be several vendors who advertise in your local paper. Many magazines have a section that lists all the products advertised in that particular issue. The components and products are categorized and listed by page number. This makes it very easy to find what you are looking for. Another source of computer information can be found in the computer books published by TAB Books and McGraw-Hill, among others.

Recommended computer magazines

The following are just a few of the magazines that can help you keep abreast to some degree.

Byte
P.O. Box 558
Highstown, N.J. 08520-9409

MicroTimes
5951 Canning St.
Oakland, CA 94609

Compute!
P.O. Box 3244
Harlan, IA 51593-2424

PC Magazine
P.O. Box 51524
Boulder CO 80321-1524

Computer Currents
5720 Hollis St.
Emeryville, CA 94608

PC Computing
P.O. Box 50253
Boulder, CO 80321-0253

Computer Graphics World
P.O. Box 122
Tulsa, OK 74101-9966

PC Sources
P.O. Box 50237
Boulder, CO 80321-0237

Computer Monthly
P.O. Box 7062
Atlanta, GA 30357-0062

PC Today
P.O. Box 85380
Lincoln, NE 68501-9815

Computer Shopper
P.O. Box 51020
Boulder CO 80321-1020

PC World
P.O. Box 51833
Boulder, CO 80321-1833

Data Based Advisor
P.O. Box 3735
Escondido, CA 92025-9895

Personal Workstation
P.O. Box 51615
Boulder, CO 80321-1615

Home Office Computing
P.O. Box 51344
Boulder, CO 80321-1344

Publish!
P.O. Box 51966
Boulder, CO 80321-1966

LAN
P.O. Box 50047
Boulder, CO 80321-0047

Unix World
P.O. Box 1929
Marion, OH 43306

Free magazines to qualified subscribers

The magazines listed in this section as free are sent only to qualified subscribers. The subscription price of a magazine usually does not cover publication, mailing, distribution, and other costs. Most magazines depend almost entirely on advertisers for their existence. The more subscribers that a magazine has, the more it can charge for its ads. Naturally magazines can attract a lot more subscribers if they are free.

PC Week and *InfoWorld* are excellent magazines. They are so popular that the publishers have to limit the number of subscribers. They cannot possibly accommodate all the people who have applied. They have set standards that have to be met in order to qualify. They do not publish the standards, so even if you answer all of the questions on the application, you still might not qualify.

To get a free subscription, you must write to the magazine for a qualifying application form. The form will ask several questions, such as how you are involved with computers, the company you work for, whether you have any influence in purchasing the computer products listed in the magazines, and several other questions that give them a very good profile of you.

The list of magazines below is not nearly complete. There are hundreds of trade magazines that are sent free to qualified subscribers. The Cahners Company alone publishes 32 different trade magazines. Many of the trade magazines are highly technical and narrowly specialized.

Automatic I.D. News
P.O. Box 6170
Duluth, MN 55806-9870

California Business
P.O. Box 70735
Pasadena, CA 91117-9947

Communications Week
P.O. Box 2070
Manhasset, NY 11030

InfoWorld Direct
401 Edgewater Place, #630
Wakefield, MA 01880

Computer Design
P.O. Box 3466
Tulsa, OK 74101-3466

Computer Products
P.O. Box 14000
Dover, NJ 07801-9990

Computer Reseller News
P.O. Box 2040
Manhasset, NY 11030

Computer Systems News
600 Community Dr.
Manhasset, NY 11030

Computer Technology Review
924 Westwood Blvd., Suite 650
Los Angeles, CA 90024-2910

Designfax
P.O. Box 1151
Skokie, IL 60076-9917

Discount Merchandiser
215 Lexington Ave.
New York, NY 10157

EE Product News
P.O. Box 12982
Overland Park, KS 66212-9817

Electronic Manufacturing
P.O. Box 159
Libertyville, IL 60048-9989

Electronic Publishing and Printing
650 S. Clark St.
Chicago, IL 60605-9960

Electronics
P.O. Box 985061
Cleveland, OH 44198-5061

Federal Computer Week
P.O. Box 602
Winchester, MA 01890-9948

ID Systems
P.O. Box 874
Peterborough, NH 03458-0874

Identification Journal
2640 N. Halsted S
Chicago, IL 60614-9962

InfoWorld
1060 Marsh Rd.
Menlo Park, CA 94025

LAN Times
122 East 1700 South
Provo, UT 84606

Lasers & Optronics
301 Gibraltar Dr.
Morris Plains, NJ 07950-9827

Machine Design
P.O. Box 985015
Cleveland, OH 44198-5015

Manufacturing Systems
P.O. Box 3008
Wheaton, IL 60189-9972

Medical Equipment Designer
29100 Aurora Rd., #200
Cleveland, OH 44139

Mini-Micro Systems
P.O. Box 5051
Denver, CO 80217-9872

Modern Office Technology
1100 Superior Ave.
Cleveland, OH 44197-8032

Office Systems 90
P.O. Box 3116
Woburn, MA 01888-9878

Office Systems Dealer 90
P.O. Box 2281
Woburn, MA 01888-9873

PC Week
P.O. Box 5920
Cherry Hill, NJ 08034

Photo Business
1515 Broadway
New York, NY 10036

The Programmer's Shop
5 Pond Park Rd.
Hingham, MA 02043-9845

Quality
P.O. Box 3002
Wheaton, IL 60189-9929

Reseller Management
P.O. Box 601
Morris, Plains, NJ 07950-9811

Robotics World
6255 Barfield Rd.
Atlanta, GA 30328-9988

Scientific Computing and Automation
301 Gibraltar Dr.
Morris Plains, NJ 07950-0608

Surface Mount Technology
P.O. Box 159
Libertyville, IL 60048-9989

Unix Review
P.O. Box 7439
San Francisco, CA 94120-7439

Public domain and shareware software

Several companies provide public domain, shareware, and low-cost software. They also publish catalogs listing their software. Some charge a small fee for their catalog.

• PC-Sig 1030D	(800) 245-6717
• MicroCom Systems	(408) 737-9000
• Public Brand Software	(800) 426-3475
• Software Express/Direct	(800) 331-8192

- Selective Software   (800) 423-3556
- The Computer Room   (703) 832-3341
- Softwarehouse   (408) 748-0461
- PC Plus Consulting   (818) 891-7930
- Micro Star   (800) 443-6103
- International Software Library (800) 992-1992
- National PD Library   (619) 941-0925
- Computers International   (619) 630-0055
- Shareware Express   (800) 346-2842

Computer books

There are several companies that publish computer books. One of the larger companies is TAB Books, Blue Ridge Summit, PA 17294-0850; (800) 822-8138. Call or write to them for a catalog of the many computer books they publish. I highly recommend them .

Chapter 16

Troubleshooting

If you assembled your computer properly, it should work perfectly. But there is always the possibility that something was not plugged in correctly or some minor error was made.

The number one cause of problems

I have a friend who works for a large computer mail-order firm. His job is to check and repair all of the components that are returned by customers. I asked him what the biggest problem was and his answer was, "People just don't read and follow the instructions or they make errors and don't check their work."

By far the greatest problem in assembling a unit or adding something to a computer is not following the instructions. Quite often it is not necessarily the fault of the person trying to follow the instructions. I have worked in the electronics industry for over 30 years, but sometimes I have great difficulty trying to decipher and follow the instructions in some manuals. Sometimes a very critical instruction or piece of information is inconspicuously buried on page 300 of a 450-page manual.

If you have just assembled your computer or added something to it, turn it on and check it out before you put the cover on. Before you turn it on, though, recheck all the cables, boards, and chips. Make sure that they are seated properly and in the right place. Read the instructions again, then turn on the power. If it works, then put the cover on and button it up. If you added a board or some accessory and your computer doesn't work, remove the item and try the computer again.

Levels of troubleshooting

There are many levels of troubleshooting. Advanced troubleshooting requires sophisticated equipment such as oscilloscopes, digital meters, logic probes, signal generators, and lots of training. But most problems will be rather minor so you don't need all that equipment and training. Most problems can be solved with just a little common sense and the use of your five senses—sight, hearing, touch, smell, and taste. Actually, you probably won't use taste very often.

Electricity—the life blood of the computer

Troubleshooting is a little easier if you know just a little of the electronic basics. Computers are possible because of electricity. An electric charge is formed when there is an imbalance or an excess amount of electrons at one pole. The excess electrons flow through whatever path they can find to get to ground or to the other pole. It is much like water flowing downhill to find its level.

Most electric or electronic paths have varying amounts of resistance so that work or heat is created when the electrons pass through them. For instance, if a flashlight is turned on, electrons pass through the bulb, which has a resistive element. The heat generated by the electrons passing through the bulb causes it to glow red hot and create light. If the light is left on for a period of time, all the excess electrons from the positive anode of the battery pass through the bulb to the negative pole of the battery. At that time, the amount of electrons at the negative and positive poles is the same. There is a perfect balance and the battery is dead.

A computer is made up of circuits and boards that have resistors, capacitors, inductors, transistors, motors, and many other components. These components perform a useful function when electricity passes through them. The circuits are designed so that the paths of the electric current are divided, controlled, and shunted to do the work that we want done.

Occasionally, too many electrons find their way through a weakened component and burn it out or for some reason, the electrons might be shunted through a different path. This might cause an intermittent, a partial, or a complete failure.

The basic components of a computer

The early IBM PC had an 8088 CPU and four other basic support chips. There were the 8259 interrupt controller, the 8237 DMA controller, the 8253/8254 programmable interval timer, and the 8255 programmable input/output controller. These same chips are found in the 8086, 80286, 80386SX, 80386DX, and the 80486. You will find two DMA controllers and two interrupt controllers in the 286, 386, and 486. You might not be able to see these chips on some motherboards, especially baby motherboards, because they are usually integrated into a large VLSI package.

The CPU is the brain of the computer. It controls the basic operation by sending and receiving control signals and memory addresses. It sends and receives data along the bus to and from other parts of the system. It carries out computations, numeric comparisons, and many other functions in response to software programs.

The 8259 programmable interrupt controller responds to interrupt requests generated by the system hardware components. These requests can be from such components as the keyboard, disk drive controller, and system timer.

The 8237 DMA controller is able to transfer data to and from the computer's memory without passing it through the CPU. This allows input/output from the disk drives without CPU involvement.

The 8253/8254 programmable interval timer generates timing signals for various system tasks. The 8255 programmable input/output controller provides an interface between the CPU and I/O devices.

Of course, several other chips are interrelated to each of these main chips and all of the main chips are interrelated. Because they are all so intimately interrelated, a failure in any main chip (and some minor chips) can cause the whole circuit to fail. The actual defect can be very difficult to pinpoint.

Fewer bugs today

In the early days of computing, there were lots of bugs and errors in clone computers. Manufacturers didn't spend a lot of money on quality control and testing. Most computer manufacturers have been making parts long enough now, however, that the designs have been firmed up and most of the bugs eliminated.

Document the problem, write it down

The chances are if your computer is going to break down, it will do it at the most inopportune time. This is one of the basic tenets of Murphy's law. If it breaks down, try not to panic. Ranting, cussing, and crying might make you feel better, but it won't solve the problem. Under no circumstances should you beat on your computer with a chair or ball bat.

Instead, get out a pad and pencil and write down everything as it happens. It is very easy to forget. Write down all the particulars, how the cables are plugged in, the software that is running, and anything that might be pertinent. You might get error messages on your screen. Use the Prt Scr (print screen) key to print out the messages.

If you can't solve the problem, you might have to call a friend or your vendor for help. If you have all the information written down, it will help. If possible, try to call from your computer as it is acting up.

Power on self-test

Every time you turn your computer on, it does a power on self-test (POST). It checks the RAM, the floppy drives, the hard disk drives, the monitor, the printer, the keyboard, and other peripherals that you have installed. If it does not find a unit, or if the unit is not functioning correctly, it will beep and display an error code. The codes start with 100 and go up to 2500 (see Table 16-1). Ordinarily the codes will not be displayed if there is no problem. If there is a problem, the last two digits of the code will be something other than 00. Each BIOS manufacturer develops their own codes so there are some slight differences.

DOS has several other error messages if you try to make the computer do something it can't do, but many of the messages are not very clear. The DOS manual explains some of them, but it doesn't give too much detail

Power supply

Most of the components in your computer are fairly low power and low voltage. The only high voltage in your system is in the power supply and it is pretty well enclosed, so there is no danger of shock if you open your computer and put your hand inside it. But you should NEVER EVER connect or disconnect a board or cable while the power is on. Fragile semiconductors might be destroyed if you do so.

Most of the power supplies have short-circuit protection. If too much of a load is placed on them, they will drop out and shut down, similar to what happens when a circuit breaker is overloaded. Most of the power supplies are designed to operate only with a load. If you take one out of a system and turn it on without a load, it will not work. You can plug in a floppy drive to act as a load if you want to check the voltages out of the system.

The fan in the power supply should provide all the cooling needed. Don't put anything around the power supply that could shut off its circulation. It could overheat. Heat is an enemy of semiconductors, so try to give the power supply plenty of breathing room.

Table 16-1. POST codes.

101	Motherboard failure
109	Direct memory access test error
121	Unexpected hardware interrupt occurred
163	Time and date not set
199	User-indicated configuration not correct
201	Memory test failure
301	Keyboard test failure or a stuck key
401	Monochrome display and/or adapter test failure
432	Parallel printer not turned on
501	Color graphics display and/or adapter test failure
601	Diskette drives and/or adapter test failure
701	Math coprocessor test error
901	Parallel printer adapter test failure
1101	Asynchronous communications adapter test failure
1301	Game control adapter test failure
1302	Joystick test failure
1401	Printer test failure
1701	Fixed disk drive and/or adapter test failure
2401	Enhanced graphics display and/or adapter test failure
2501	Enhanced graphics display and/or adapter test failure

The semiconductors in your computer have no moving parts. If they were designed properly, they should last indefinitely. Heat is an enemy and can cause semiconductor failure. The fan in the power supply should provide adequate cooling. All the openings on the back panel that correspond to the slots on the motherboard should have fillers. Even the holes on the bottom of the chassis should be covered with tape. This forces the fan to draw air in from the front of the computer, pull it over the boards, and exhaust it through the opening in the power supply case. Nothing should be placed in front or behind the computer that will restrict air flow. If you don't hear the fan when you turn on your computer, then the power supply could be defective.

The eight-slotted connectors on the motherboard have 62 contacts—31 on the A side and 31 on the B side. The black ground wires connect to B1 of each of the eight slots. B3 and B29 have +5 Vdc, B5 has –5 Vdc, B7 has –12 Vdc, and B9 has +12 Vdc. These voltages go to the listed pins on each of the eight plug-in slots (see Table 16-2).

Instruments and tools

For high levels of troubleshooting you need some rather sophisticated and expensive instruments. You need a good high-frequency oscilloscope, a digital analyzer, a logic probe, and several other expensive pieces of gear. You also need a test bench with a power supply, disk drives, and a computer with some empty slots so that you can plug in suspect boards and test them.

You also need a volt-ohmmeter, some clip leads, side-cutting dikes, long-nose pliers, various screwdrivers, nut drivers, a soldering iron and solder, and lots of differ-

Table 16-2. Power supply connections.

Disk drive power supply connections

Pin	Color	Function
1	Yellow	+12-V dc
2	Black	Ground
3	Black	Ground
4	Red	+5-V dc

Power supply connections to the motherboard

	Pin	Color	Function
P8			
	1	White	Power good
	2	No connection	
	3	Yellow	+12-V dc
	4	Brown	−12-V dc
	5	Black	Ground
	6	Black	Ground
P9			
	1	Black	Ground
	2	Black	Ground
	3	Blue	−5-V dc
	4	Red	+5-V dc
	5	Red	+5-V dc
	6	Red	+5-V dc

ent size screws and nuts. You need plenty of light over the bench and a flashlight or a small light to light up the dark places in the case. And most importantly, you need quite a lot of training and experience. But for many problems, just a little common sense will tell you what is wrong.

Common problems

Most common problems don't require a lot of test gear, just your eyes, ears, nose, and touch:

- Eyes—If you look closely, you can see a cable that is not plugged in properly, or a board that is not completely seated, or a switch that is not set right, and many other obvious things.

- Ears—You can use your ears for any unusual sounds. The only sound from your computer should be the noise of your drive motors and the fan in the power supply.

- Smell—If you have ever smelled a burned resistor or capacitor, you will never forget it. If you smell something very unusual, try to locate where it is coming from.

- Touch—If you touch a component and it seems unusually hot, it could be the cause of your problem. Except for the insides of your power supply, there should not be any voltage above 12 volts in your computer. It should be safe to touch the components.

Electrostatic discharge (ESD)

Before you touch any of the components or handle them, you should ground yourself and discharge any static voltage that you have built up. You can discharge yourself by touching an unpainted metal part on the case of a computer or other device that is plugged in. It is possible for a person to build up a charge of 4000 volts or more of electrostatic voltage. If you walk across a carpet and then touch a brass door knob, you can sometimes see a spark fly and will get a shock. Most electronic assembly lines have the workers wear a ground strap whenever they are working with ESD-sensitive components.

Recommended tools

You should have the following tools around the house, even if you never have any computer problems.

- Several sizes of screwdrivers. A couple of them should be magnetic for picking up and starting small screws. You can buy magnetic screwdrivers or you can make them yourself. Rub the blade of the screwdriver a few times on a strong magnet. The magnets on cabinet doors will do, or the voice coil magnet of a loud speaker. Be very careful with any magnet around your floppy diskettes; it can erase them.

- A small screwdriver with a bent tip that can be used to pry up ICs. Some of the larger ICs are very difficult to remove. One of the blank fillers for the slots on the back panel also makes a good prying tool.

- A couple of different pliers. You should have at least one long-nose pliers.

- Side-cutting dikes for clipping leads of components and cutting wire. You can buy cutters that also have wire strippers.

- A soldering iron and solder. You shouldn't have to do any soldering but you never know when you might need it. A soldering iron can come in handy around the house.

- A volt-ohmmeter. They can be used to check for the correct wiring in house wall sockets (the wide slot should be ground), to check switches, to check wiring continuity in your car, house, stereo, and phone lines, and you can check for the proper voltages in your computer. There are only four voltages to check for— +12 volts, –12 volts, +5 volts, and –5 volts. You can buy a relatively inexpensive volt-ohmmeter at any Radio Shack or electronics stores.

- Clip leads. You can buy these at your local Radio Shack or electronics store.
- A flashlight for looking into the dark places inside the computer.

How to find the problem

If you suspect a board, and you have a spare or can borrow one, swap it. If you suspect a board, but don't know which one, take the boards out to the barest minimum and add them back until the problem develops.

CAUTION: Always turn off the power when plugging in or unplugging a board or cable. Wiggle the boards and cables to see if it is an intermittent problem. Often, a wire is broken but still makes contact until it is moved.

Check the ICs and connectors for bent pins. If you have installed memory ICs and get errors, check to make sure that they are seated properly and that all the pins are in the sockets. If you swap an IC, make a note of how it is oriented before removing it. There should be a small dot of white paint or a U-shaped indentation at the end that has pin 1. If you forgot to note the orientation, look at the other ICs. Most of the boards are laid out so that all of the ICs are oriented the same way. The chrome fillers that are used to cover the unused slots in the back of the case make very good tools for prying up ICs.

You might also try unplugging a cable or a board and plugging it back in. Sometimes the pins might be slightly corroded or not seated properly. Before unplugging a cable, you should put a stripe on the connector and cable with a marking pen or nail polish so that you can easily see how they should be plugged back in.

The problem could be in a DIP switch. You might try turning it on and off a few times.

CAUTION: Always make a diagram of the wires, cables, and switch settings before you disturb them. It is easy to forget how they were plugged in or set before you moved them. You could end up making things worse. Make a pencil mark before turning a knob, variable coil, or capacitor so that it can be returned to the same setting when you discover that it didn't help. Better yet, resist the temptation to reset these types of components. Most were set using highly sophisticated instruments. They don't usually change enough to cause a problem.

If you are having monitor problems, check the switch settings on the motherboard. There are several different motherboards. Some have DIP switches or shorting bars that must be set to configure the system for monochrome, CGA, EGA, or VGA. Most monitors also have fuses. You might check them and the cables for proper connections.

Printer problems, especially serial type, are so numerous that I will not even attempt to list them here. Many printers today have parallel and serial ports. The IBM defaults to the parallel system. If at all possible, use the parallel port. There are very few problems with parallel as compared to serial. Most printers have a self-test. The printer might run this test fine, but then completely ignore any efforts to get it to respond to the computer if the cables, parity, and baud rate are not properly set.

Sometimes the computer will hang up if you tell it to do something that it can't do. You can usually do a warm reboot of the computer by pressing Ctrl-Alt-Del. Of course, this will wipe out any file in memory that you might have been working on. Occasionally the computer will not respond to a warm boot. You can pound on the keyboard all day long and it will ignore you. In this case, you have to switch off the main power, let it sit for a few seconds, then power up again. Always wait for the hard disk to wind down and stop before turning the power on again.

Diagnostic and utility software

When IBM came out with the XT, they developed a diagnostic or setup disk that was included with every machine. It checked the keyboard, disk drives, monitor, and peripherals, and other tests. When the AT was released, the diagnostic disk was revised a bit to include even more tests. You had to have the disk to set the time, date, and all the other on-board CMOS system configurations.

Most BIOS chips now have many of the diagnostic routines built-in. These routines allow you to set the time and date, tell the computer what type of hard drive and floppies are installed, the amount of memory, the wait states, and several other functions. AMI and DTK BIOS chips have a very comprehensive set of built-in diagnostics. They can allow hard and floppy disk formatting, check the speed of rotation of the disk drives, do performance testing of hard drives, and several other tests.

I mentioned these utility software programs in chapter 14. Many of them have a few diagnostics among the utilities.

- Norton Utilities—includes several diagnostic and test programs such as Disk Doctor, Disk Test, Format Recover, Directory Sort, System Information, and others.

- Mace Utilities—does about everything that Norton does and a few other things. It has recover, defragment, diagnose, remedy, and several other very useful functions primarily for the hard disk.

- PC Tools—has several utilities much like the Norton and Mace Utilities. It has a utility that can recover data from a disk that has been erased or reformatted. It has several other data recovery and DOS utilities. It can be used for hard disk backup and has several utilities such as those found in Side-Kick.

- SpinRite, Disk Technician, OPTune, and DOSUTILS—utilities that allow you to diagnose, analyze, and optimize your hard disk.

- CheckIt—checks and reports on your computer configuration by letting "you look inside your PC without taking off the cover." It reports on the type of processor, amount of memory, video adapter, hard and floppy drives, clock/calendar, ports, keyboard, and mouse (if present). It also tests the motherboard, hard and floppy disks, RAM, ports, keyboard, mouse, joysticks, and other tests. It can also run a few benchmark speed tests.

There are several other diagnostic software and hardware tools. Check the ads in computer magazines.

What to do if it is completely dead

Software diagnostics are great in many cases, but if the computer is completely dead, the software won't do you any good. If it is completely dead, the first thing to do is check the power. If you don't have a voltmeter, plug a lamp in the same socket and see if it lights. Check your power cord. Check the switch on the computer. Check the fan in the power supply. Is it turning? Check the monitor, its power cord, its fuses, and its adapter. If these all seem to be okay, then you probably have some serious problems. You probably need some high-level troubleshooting.

Software problems

I have had far more trouble with software than I have had with hardware. Quite often it is my fault for not taking the time to completely read the manuals and instructions. For instance, I tried to install Charisma. It is a large program and works under Windows. I kept getting errors and it would not load. I finally read the manual and found that it requires at least 500K of memory to install. I have several drivers, TSRs, and other things in my config.sys file that eats up a lot or RAM. I had to boot up with a plain diskette that had a very simple config.sys file that left me over 500K of RAM. I had no trouble after that. Prodigy and several other large programs also need about 500K of RAM in order to run.

MS-DOS 5.0, DR-DOS 6.0, DESQview, and several other programs can load drivers, TSRs, and other things into memory above 640K. This can leave as much as 630K of free RAM. Windows 3.0 comes with a HIMEM.SYS file that is necessary for accessing extended memory. This file is loaded with the config.sys file. If HIMEM.SYS is loaded, it will conflict with the DR-DOS high-memory files. You can run one or the other, but if both are loaded, the computer will not boot.

There are thousands of other software problems that you will probably run into. Many vendors have support programs for their products. If something goes wrong, you can call them. A few of them offer toll-free numbers. With most of them, you have to pay for the call and some companies charge for their support. Some have installed 900 telephone numbers. You are charged a certain amount for the amount of time you are on the phone.

If you have a software problem, document everything that happens. Before you call, try to duplicate the problem or make it happen again. Carefully read the manual. When you call, it is best to be in front of your computer, with it turned on, and with the problem on the screen if possible. Also before you call, have the serial number of your program handy. One of the first things they will probably ask is your name and serial number. If you bought and registered the program, it will be in their computer.

There are still compatibility problems with updates and new releases of software. I had lots of problems trying to get the latest WordStar release to work with files I created with an earlier version. It was mostly my fault because I didn't take the time to read the manual. Like so many other updates and revisions, they make them bigger and better, but out of necessity, they often change the way things are done.

Most software programs are reasonably bug-free, but there are millions of things that can go wrong if the exact instructions and procedures are not followed. In many cases, the exact instructions and procedures are not very explicit.

Hardware problems

There are many things that can go wrong with hardware also. Some things might happen once and never again. For instance, my 3½-inch drive had been working perfectly. I tried to load a program and it gave me the DOS error message, Sector not found, error reading drive B:. I thought maybe I had screwed up my program diskette, so I tried it on one of my other computers and it worked fine. I pulled the drive out and took the cover off. I hooked it up and tried to read a diskette, but I could see that the head never moved. The head is attached to a long, screw-type worm gear. The head actuator motor turns the screw and moves the head to the various tracks. I turned the power off and moved the head manually. It seemed to be stuck at first, but then it moved freely. I turned the power back on and it worked perfectly. I have not had any trouble since and it will probably never happen again.

I took my 486 to a user group meeting and demonstrated how easy it was to assemble one. When I got back home, neither of my floppy drives would operate. Because neither would operate, I figured it could be the cable or the floppy controller portion of my hard disk controller. I installed a new cable, but it didn't help. I then plugged in a new floppy controller, and still could not read or write to the floppies. Then I really began to worry; maybe I had damaged my $4450 motherboard when I transported it to the meeting.

It didn't seem logical that both floppy drives could be bad, but I disconnected them and plugged in another 1.2Mb drive. It worked perfectly. I then reinstalled the 1.44Mb drive and it worked also. It seems that whatever was wrong with the 1.2Mb A drive also kept the B drive from operating. I had evidently damaged it in handling. I was unhappy that it was only a $60 floppy drive and not my very expensive motherboard. Because it would cost more to troubleshoot and repair than it was worth, I scrapped the drive and bought a new one.

Computers are very unforgiving. It is very easy to plug a cable in backwards or forget to set a switch. Sometimes it is difficult to determine if it is a hardware problem caused by software or vice versa. There is no way that every problem can abe addressed, but there are several common-sense things that you can do to solve many of your problems.

One of the best ways to find answers is to ask someone who has had the same problem. One of the best places to find those people is at a users group. If at all possible, join one. You can also get help from local bulletin boards. Your computer is not complete without a modem so that you can contact them.

Several local computer magazines list user groups and bulletin boards as a service to their readers. The nationally published *Computer Shopper* prints a very comprehensive list each month. There are thousands of things that can go wrong. Sometimes it could be a combination of both software and hardware. Sometimes there is only one way to do something the right way, but ten thousand ways to do it wrong.

Is it worth repairing?

If you find a problem on a board, a disk drive, or some component you should compare the cost of replacing it versus having it repaired. With low-cost clone hardware available, it is often less expensive to scrap a defective part and buy a new one. Again, if at all possible, join a users group and become friendly with all of the members. They can be one of your best sources of information when troubleshooting. Most of them have had similar problems and are glad to help.

A personal letter

Dear Friend,

I want to thank you for buying my book. I want to write a book on troubleshooting. You can help me. Please take a few minutes and write down any problems that you have experienced and tell me how you solved them, if they were solved.

Please send your notes to Aubrey Pilgrim, c/o TAB Books, Blue Ridge Summit, PA 17294-0850.

Thank you.
Aubrey

Glossary

access time   The amount of time it takes the computer to find and read data from a disk or from memory. The average access time for a hard disk is based on the time it takes the head to seek and find the specified track, to lock onto it, and for the disk to spin around until the desired sector is beneath the head.

active partition   The partition on a hard disk that contains the boot and operating system. A single hard disk can be partitioned into several logical disks such as drive C, drive D, and drive E. This can be done at the initial formatting of the disk. Only one partition, usually drive C, can contain the active partition.

adapter boards or cards   The plug-in boards needed to drive monitors. Monitor boards can be monochrome graphic adapters (MGA), color graphic adapters (CGA), enhanced graphic adapters (EGA), or video graphic adapters (VGA).

algorithm   A step-by-step procedure, scheme, formula, or method used to solve a problem or accomplish a task. Might be a subroutine in a software program.

alphanumeric   Data that has both numerals and letters.

analyst   A person who determines the computer needs to accomplish a given task. The job of an analyst is similar to that of a consultant. Note that there are no standard qualifications for either of these jobs. Anyone can call himself an analyst or a consultant.

ANSI   American National Standard Institute. A standard adopted by MS-DOS for cursor positioning. It is used in the ANSI.SYS file for device drivers.

ASCII   American Standard Code for Information Interchange. Binary numbers from 0 to 127 represent the upper- and lowercase letters of the alphabet, the numbers 0 through 9, and the several symbols found on a keyboard. A block of eight 0s and 1s are used to represent all of these characters. The first 32 characters, 0 through 31, are reserved for noncharacter functions of a keyboard, modem, printer, or other device. Number 32, or 0010 000, represents the space, which is a character. The numeral 1 is represented by the binary number for 49, which is 0011 0001. Text written in ASCII is displayed on the computer screen as standard text. Text written in other systems, such as WordStar, has several other characters added and is very difficult to read. Another 128 character representations were added to the original 128 for graphics and programming purposes.

ASIC   Application Specific Integrated Circuit.

assembly language   A low-level machine language made up of 0s and 1s.

asynchronous   A serial type of communication where one bit at a time is transmitted. The bits are usually sent in blocks of eight 0s and 1s.

AT-type systems   The 286, 386SX, 386DX, and 486 are all based on the original IBM AT-type, 16-bit bus.

autoexec.bat   If present, this file is run automatically by DOS after it boots up. It is a file that you can configure to suit your own needs. It can load and run certain programs or configure your system.

baby motherboards   AT-type motherboards that have been shrunk to the size of the XT by combining and integrating several of the chips.

.BAK files   Anytime you edit or change a file in some of the word processors and other software programs, the program saves the original file as a backup and appends the extension .BAK to it.

BASIC   Beginners All-Purpose Symbolic Instruction Code. A high-level language that was once very popular. There are still many programs and games that use it. BASIC programs usually have a .BAS extension.

batch   The batch command can be used to link commands and run them automatically. Batch commands can be made up by the user. They all have the extension .bat.

baud   A measurement of the speed or data transfer rate of a communications line between the computer and the printer, modem, or another computer.

benchmark   A standard program against which similar programs can be compared.

bidirectional   Both directions. Most printers print in both directions, thereby saving the time it takes to return to the other end of a line.

binary   Binary numbers are 0s and 1s.

BIOS   Basic Input/Output System. The BIOS is responsible for handling all input/output operations.

bit-mapped   The representation of a video image stored in the computer memory. Fonts for alphanumeric characters are usually stored as bit maps. When the letter A is typed, the computer goes to its library and pulls out a preformed A and sends it to the monitor. If a different size A, or font, is needed, it requires another bit-map set. Graphic images can also be bit-mapped. They consume an enormous amount of memory. Newer techniques allow different sizes and types of fonts to be scaled rather than bit-mapped. *See* typeface.

bits   Binary digits.

boot or bootstrap   When a computer is turned on, all the memory and other internal operators have to be set or configured. A small amount of the program to do this is stored in ROM. Using this, the computer pulls itself up by its boot straps. A warm boot is sometimes necessary to get the computer out of an endless loop, or if it is hung up for some reason. A warm boot can be done by pressing Ctrl-Alt-Del.

buffer   A buffer is usually some discrete amount of memory used to hold data. A computer can send data thousands of times faster than a printer or modem can utilize it. The data can be input to a buffer, which can then feed the data into the printer as needed. The computer is then free to do other tasks.

bug, debug   The early computers were made with high-voltage vacuum tubes. It took rooms full of hot tubes to do the job that a credit card calculator can do today. One of the large systems went down one day. After several hours of troubleshooting, the technicians found a large bug had crawled into the high-voltage wiring. It had been electrocuted and had shorted out the whole system. Since that time, any type of trouble in a piece of software or hardware is called a bug. To debug it, of course, is to try to find all of the errors or defects.

bulletin boards   Usually a computer with a hard disk that can be accessed with a modem. Software and programs can be uploaded or left on the bulletin board by a caller, or a caller can scan the software that has been left there by others and download any that he likes. Bulletin boards often have help and message services. A great source of help for a beginner.

burst mode   The bus is taken over and a packet of data is sent as a single unit. During this time the bus cannot be accessed by other requests until the burst operation is completed. This allows 33Mb per second or more to be transmitted over the bus.

bus Wires or circuits that connect a number of devices together. It can also be a system. The configuration of the circuits that connect the 62 pins of the 8 slots together on the motherboard is a bus.

byte A byte is eight bits, or a block of eight 0s and 1s. These 8 bits can be arranged in 256 different ways. This is $2\times2\times2\times2\times2\times2\times2\times2\times2=256$, or 2^8. Therefore, one byte can be made to represent any one of the 256 characters in the ASCII character set. It takes one byte to make a single character. There are four characters in the word byte and it requires four bytes, or 32 bits.

cache memory May be a disk cache or a high-speed memory cache. A high-speed buffer set up in memory to hold data that is being read from the hard disks. Often a program will request the same data from the disk over and over again. This can be quite time-consuming, depending on the access speed of the disk drive and the location of the data on the disk. If the requested data is cached in memory it can be accessed almost immediately.

For some of the very fast 386 and 486 systems, the DRAM is too slow to keep up, so a cache of very fast SRAM might be installed for these systems.

carriage width The width of a typewriter or printer. The two standard widths are 80 columns and 132 columns.

cell A place for a single unit of data in memory or an address in a spreadsheet.

Centronics parallel port A system of 8-bit parallel transmission first used by the Centronics Company. It has become a standard and is the default method of printer output on the IBM.

character A letter, a number, or an 8-bit piece of data.

chip An integrated circuit, usually made from a silicon wafer. It can be microscopically etched and have thousands of transistors and semiconductors in a very small area.

CISC Complex Instruction Set Computing. This is the standard type of computer design as opposed to the reduced instruction set computers (RISC) used in larger systems. It might require as many as six steps for a CISC system to carry out a command. An RISC system might need only two steps to perform a similar function.

clock The operations of a computer are based on very critical timing. They use a crystal to control their internal clocks. The standard frequency for the PC and XT is 4.77 MHz. The turbo systems operate at 6 MHz to 8 MHz.

cluster Each track of a disk is divided into sectors. Two or more sectors are called a cluster. This term has been replaced by the term **allocation unit**. An allocation unit can be one or more sectors.

COM Usually refers to serial ports COM1 and COM2. These ports are used for serial printers, modems, mice, plotters, and other serial devices.

.COM A .COM or .EXE extension on the end of a file name indicates that it is a program that can run commands to execute programs.

COMMAND.COM An essential command that must be present in order to boot and start the computer.

COMDEX Computer Dealers Exposition. The nation's largest computer exposition and show, usually held once in the spring in Atlanta or Chicago and in the fall in Las Vegas.

composite video A less expensive monitor that combines all the colors in a single input line.

console In the early days a monitor and keyboard were set up at a desklike console. The term has stuck. A console is a computer. The command COPY CON allows you to use the keyboard as a typewriter. Type COPY CON PRN or COPY CON LPT1 and everything you type will be sent to the printer. At the end of your file, use Ctrl-Z or F6 to stop sending.

consultant Someone who is supposed to be an expert who can advise you and help you determine what your computer needs are. Similar to an analyst. There are no standard requirements or qualifications that must be met. Anyone can call himself an analyst or consultant.

conventional memory Also called **real memory**. The first 640K of RAM, the memory that DOS handles. The memory actually consists of 1Mb, but the 384K above the 640K is reserved for system use.

coprocessor Usually an 8087, 80287, or 80387 that works in conjunction with the CPU and vastly speeds up some operations.

copy protection A system that prevents a diskette from being copied.

cps Characters Per Second. When referring to a printer, the speed that it can print.

CPU Central Processing Unit. The Intel 8088, 80286, 80386, or 80486.

CRT A cathode-ray tube. The large tube that is the screen of computer monitors and TVs.

CSMA/CD Carrier Sense Multiple Access with Collision Detection. A network system that controls the transmissions from several nodes. It detects if two stations try to send at the same time and notifies the senders to try again at random times.

current directory The directory of files that are in use at the time.

cursor The blinking spot on the screen that indicates where the next character will be input.

daisywheel A round printer or typewriter wheel with flexible fingers that have the alphabet and other formed characters. A solenoid driven hammer hits the assigned character and presses it against a ribbon onto the paper. Daisywheel printers can provide excellent letter quality type, but are very slow.

database A collection of data, usually related in some way.

DATE command The date can be displayed anytime DATE is typed at the prompt sign.

DES Data Encryption Standard. First developed by IBM. It can be used to encrypt data so that it is almost impossible to decode it unless you have the code.

DIP Dual Inline Pins. Refers to the two rows of pins on the sides of most IC chips.

disk controller A plug-in board that is used to control the hard and/or floppy disk drives. All of the read and write signals go through the controller.

DMA Direct Memory Access. Some parts of the computer, such as the disk drives, can exchange data directly with the RAM without having to go through the CPU.

documentation Manuals, instructions, or specifications for a system, hardware, or software.

DOS Disk Operating System. Software that allows programs to interact and run on a computer.

dot matrix   A type of printer that uses a matrix of thin wires or pins to make up the print head. Electronic solenoids push the pins out to form letters out of dots. The dots are made when the pins are pushed against the ribbon and paper.

double density   At one time, most diskettes were single-sided and had a capacity of 80K to 100K. The technology has advanced so that diskettes can be recorded on both sides with up to 200K per side. The 5¼-inch 360K, and the 3½-inch 720K diskettes are double-sided, double density. The 1.2Mb and 1.44Mb diskettes are high density.

DPMI   DOS Protected-Mode Interface. A proposed specification to govern the interaction of large applications with each other, DOS, and OS/2.

DRAM   Dynamic Random-Access Memory. This is the usual type of memory found in personal computers. It is the least expensive of memory types.

DTP   Desktop Publishing. A rather loose term that can be applied to a small personal computer and a printer as well as to high-powered sophisticated systems.

dumb terminal   A terminal that is tied to a mainframe or one that does not have its own microprocessor.

duplex   A characteristic of a communications channel that enables data to be transmitted in both directions. Full duplex allows the information to be transmitted in both directions simultaneously. In half duplex, information can be transmitted in both directions, but not at the same time.

EATA   Enhanced AT Attachment. A standard proposed by the Common Access Method (CAM) committee. Their proposal would define a standard interface for connecting controllers to PCs. It would define a standard software protocol and hardware interface for disk controllers, SCSI host adapters, and other intelligent chip-embedded controllers.

echo   A command that can cause information to be displayed on the screen from a .bat or other file. Echo can be turned on or off.

EEPROM   An Electrically Erasable Programmable Read-Only Memory.

EGA   Enhanced Graphics Adapter. Board used for high-resolution monitors.

E-Mail   Electronic Mail. A system that allows messages to be sent through LANs (local area networks) or by modem over telephone lines.

EMS   Expanded Memory Specification. A specification for adding expanded memory put forth by Lotus, Intel, and Microsoft (LIM EMS).

EPROM   An Erasable Programmable Read-Only Memory.

ergonomics   The study and science of how the human body can be the most productive in working with machinery. This includes the study of the effects monitors, chairs, lighting, and other environmental and physical factors.

errors   DOS displays several error messages if it receives bad commands or there are problems of some sort.

ESDI   Enhanced System Device Interface. A hard disk interface that allows data to be transferred to and from the disk at a rate of 10Mb per second. The older standard ST506 allowed only 5Mb per second.

.EXE   A file with this extension indicates that it is an executable file that can run and execute the program. It is similar to the .COM files.

expanded memory   Memory that can be added to a PC, XT, or AT. It can only be accessed through special software.

expansion boards A board that can be plugged into one of the eight slots on the motherboard to add memory or other functions.

extended memory RAM that can be added to an 286, 386, or 486.

external commands DOS commands that are not loaded into memory when the computer is booted.

FAT File Allocation Table. This is a table on the disk that DOS uses to keep track of all of the parts of a file. A file might be placed in sector 3 of track 1, sectors 5 and 6 of track 10, and sector 4 of track 20. The file allocation table keeps track of where the parts are located and directs the read or record head to those areas when requested to do so.

fax A shortened form of the word facsimile and X for transmission. A fax machine scans an image or textual document and digitizes it in a graphical form. As it scans an image, 0s or 1s are generated depending on the presence or absence of darkness (ink). The 0s and 1s are transmitted over the telephone line as voltages. *See* modem.

fonts Different types of print characters such as Gothic, Courier, Roman, Helvetica, and others. Each is a collection of unique characters and symbols.

format The process of preparing a disk so that it can record. The formatting process lays down tracks and sectors so that data can be written anywhere on the disk and recovered easily.

fragmentation If a disk has records that have been changed several times, there are bits of the files on several different tracks and sectors. This slows down writing and reading of the files because the head has to move to the various tracks. If these files are copied to a newly formatted disk, each file will be written to clean tracks that are contiguous. This will decrease the access time of the hard disk.

friction feed A printer that uses a roller or platen to pull the paper through.

game port An input/output port for joysticks, trackballs, paddles, and other devices.

gigabyte One billion bytes. This will be a common size memory in a very short time.

glitch An unexpected electrical spike or static disturbance that can cause a loss of data.

global A character or something that appears throughout an entire document or program.

googool A very large figure; 1 followed by 100 zeros.

GUI Graphical User Interface. It usually makes use of a mouse, icons, and windows such as those used by the Macintosh.

handshaking A protocol or routine between systems, usually the printer and the computer, to indicate a readiness to communicate with each other.

hardware The physical parts that make up a computer system such as disk drives, keyboards, monitors, etc.

Hayes compatible Hayes was one of the first modem manufacturers. Like IBM, they created a set of standards that most others have adopted.

hexadecimal A system that uses the base 16. Our binary system is based on 2; our decimal system is based on 10. The hexadecimal goes from 00, 01, 02, 03, 04, 05,

06, 07, 08, 09, 0A, 0B, 0C, 0D, 0E, 0F. Ten would be 16 in the system, and it starts over so that 20 would be 32 in decimal. Most of the computer's memory locations are in hexadecimal.

hidden files   Files that do not show up in a normal directory display, such as DOS files that are necessary to boot a computer. These are hidden so that they will not be accidentally erased.

high-level language   A language such as BASIC, Pascal, or C that is fairly easy to read and understand.

ICs   Integrated Circuits. The first integrated circuit was the placing of two transistors in a single can early in the 1960s. Then several semiconductors were placed in a package. This was called small-scale integration (SSI). This was followed by large-scale integration (LSI), then very large-scale integration (VLSI). Today we have very high-scale integrated circuits (VHSICs). We have almost run out of descriptive adjectives.

IDE   Integrated Disk Electronics. Western Digital and other companies are manufacturing hard drives with most of the controller circuitry on the disk assembly. They still need an interface of some sort to connect to the computer. They are somewhat similar to SCSI.

interface   A piece of hardware or a set of rules that allows communications between two systems.

internal commands   Those commands that are loaded into memory when DOS boots up.

interpreter   A program that translates a high-level language into machine-readable code.

ISDN   Integrated Services Distribution Network. A standard for telephone communications for transmission of voice, data, and images.

kilobyte   1000 bytes (1K). More exactly, it is 1024 bytes or 2^{10}.

LAN   Local Area Network. Several computers tied together or to a central server.

laser printer   A type of printer that uses the same type of "engine" used in copy machines. An electronically controlled laser beam sweeps across a drum. The beam leaves a static charge on the drum with an image of the letters or graphics to be printed. The charged areas of the drum then pick up toner particles and deposit them on the page. The page is routed through a heat process that fuses the toner particles to the page.

LIM-EMS   Lotus-Intel-Microsoft Expanded Memory Specification.

low-level format   Most hard disks must have a preliminary low-level format performed on them before they can be formatted for DOS. Low-level formatting is sometimes called initializing.

low-level language   A machine-level language, usually in binary digits, that is very difficult for the ordinary person to understand.

LQ   Letter Quality. The type from a daisywheel or formed type printers.

macro   A series of keystrokes that can be recorded, somewhat like a batch file, and typed back when one or more keys are pressed. For instance, I can type my entire return address with just two keystrokes.

mainframe   A large computer that can serve several users.

megabyte   1,000,000 bytes (1Mb). More precisely, it is 2^{20} or 1,048,576 bytes. It takes a minimum of 20 data lines to address 1Mb, a minimum of 24 lines (2^{24}) to address 16Mb, and a minimum of 25 lines (2^{25}) to address 32Mb.

menu   A list of choices or options. A menu-driven system makes it very easy for beginners to choose what they want to run or do.

MFM   Modified Frequency Modulation. The scheme for the standard method of recording on hard disks. *See* RLL.

MHz   Megahertz; a million cycles per second. Older technicians still call it cps. A few years ago, a committee decided to honor Heinrich Rudolf Hertz (1857–1894) for his early work in electromagnetism so they changed the cycles per second (cps) to Hertz (Hz).

modem   **Mo**modulator-**dem**modulator. A device that allows data to be sent through telephone lines. A modem creates digital voltages that are changed or modulated to an analog voltage, transmitted over the telephone lines, and demodulated by the receiving modem.

mouse   A small pointing device that controls the cursor and moves it anywhere on the screen. It has one to three buttons that are assigned various functions.

MTBF   Mean Time Before Failure. An average of the time before failure, usually used to describe a hard disk or other component.

multitasking   The ability of a computer to perform more than one task at a time. Many computers have this ability when used with the proper software.

multiuser   A computer that is capable of providing service to more than one user; such as a server for a LAN.

NEAT chip set   New Enhanced AT chip set. Chips and Technology combined the functions of several chips found on the original IBM motherboard into just a few VLSI circuits. These chips are used on the vast majority of clone boards.

NLQ   Near Letter Quality. The better formed characters from a dot matrix printer.

null modem cable   A cable with certain pairs of wires crossed over. If the computer sends data from pin 2, the modem might receive it on pin 3. The modem would send data back to the computer from its pin 2 and it is received by the computer on pin 3. Several other wires might also be crossed.

OOP   Object-Oriented Programs. A type of programming that utilizes parts of existing programs to provide new applications.

OS/2   A high-end operating system that is similar to DOS. It can be used on the 286, 386, and 486 machines.

parallel   A system that uses eight lines to send eight bits at a time, or one byte.

parity checking   In the computer memory system, it is an error detection technique that verifies the integrity of the RAM contents. This is the function of the ninth chip in a memory bank. Parity checking systems are also used in other areas such as verifying the integrity of data transmitted by a modem.

PCMCIA   Personal Computer Memory Card International Association. A standard for plug-in memory cards used in laptop computers.

plotter   An *X-Y* writing device that can be used for charts, graphics, and other functions that most printers can't do.

prompt   The > sign that shows that DOS is waiting for an entry. The prompt command can be programmed to display almost anything you want it to. If you place the command PROMPT PG in your autoexec.bat file it causes the current drive letter and current directory to be displayed.

protocol   The rules and methods by which computers and modems communicate with each other.

QIC   Quarter-Inch Cartridge. A width of tape used in tape backup systems.

RAM   Random-Access Memory. This is computer memory that is used to temporarily hold files and data as they are being worked on, changed, or altered. It can be written to and read from. It is volatile memory. Any data stored in it is lost when the power is turned off.

RGB   Red, Green, Blue. The three primary colors that are used in color monitors and TVs. Each color has its own electron gun that shoots streams of electrons to the back of the monitor display and causes it to light up in various colors.

RISC   Reduced Instruction Set Computing. A design that allows a computer to operate with fewer instructions, allowing it to run much faster.

RLL   Run Length Limited. A scheme of hard disk recording that allows 50% more data to be recorded on a hard disk than the standard MFM scheme. The MFM system divides each track into 17 sectors of 512 bytes each. The RLL format divides the tracks into 26 sectors with 512 bytes each.

ROM   Read-Only Memory. It does not change when the power is turned off. The primary use of ROM is in the system BIOS and on some plug-in boards.

scalable typeface   Unlike bit-mapped systems where each font has one size and characteristic, scalable systems allow typefaces to be shrunk or enlarged to different sizes to meet specific needs. This allows much more flexibility and uses less memory. There are also scalable graphic systems.

SCSI   Small Computer System Interface (pronounced scuzzy). A fast parallel hard disk interface system developed by Shugart Associates and adopted by the ANSI. The SCSI system allows multiple drives to be connected. It supports a parallel transfer rate of 1.2Mb per second. The ESDI serial system can send 10Mb per second, one bit at a time. Because it takes eight bits to make a byte, the ESDI and SCSI systems have about the same speed.

sector   A section of a track on a disk or diskette. A sector ordinarily holds 512 bytes. A 360K diskette has 40 tracks per side. Each track is divided into nine sectors.

serial   The transmission of one bit at a time over a single line.

shadow RAM   A technology provided on some motherboards that allows the option to copy system ROM BIOS into unused portions of high memory. Because RAM is faster than ROM, this can speed up the system.

SIMM   Single Inline Memory Module.

SIP   Single Inline Package. A memory module that has pins. Many small resistor packs and integrated circuits have a single line of pins.

source diskette   When using the DISKCOPY command, it is the original diskette to be copied from.

SPARC   Scalable Processor Architecture. A RISC system developed by Sun Microsystems for workstations.

spool   Simultaneous Peripheral Operations On-Line. A spooler acts as a storage buffer for data that is fed out to a printer or other device. It frees the computer for other tasks.

SRAM Static RAM. A type of RAM that can be much faster than DRAM. SRAM is made up of actual transistors that are turned on and off and will maintain their state without constant refreshing, such as needed in DRAM. SRAM is considerably more expensive and requires more space than DRAM.

target diskette When using the DISKCOPY command, it is the diskette to be copied to.

time stamp The record of the time and date that is recorded in the directory when a file is created or changed.

tractor A printer device with sprockets or spikes that pulls the computer paper through the printer at a very precise feed rate using the holes in the margins. A friction feed platen might allow the paper to slip, move to one side or the other, and not be precise in the spacing between the lines.

Trojan horse A harmful piece of code or software hidden in a software package that will later cause destruction. It is unlike a virus in that it does not grow and spread.

TSOP Thin Small Outline Packages. A new standard proposed for memory cards such as those used in laptops. It is about the size of a credit card.

TSR Terminate and Stay Resident. When a program such as Sidekick is loaded in memory, it will normally stay there until the computer is booted up again. If several TSR programs are loaded in memory, there might not be enough memory left to run some programs.

turbo Usually means a computer with a faster than normal speed.

UMB Upper Memory Block. Refers to the memory above 640K. With DOS versions higher than 5.0 and other memory managers such as DESQview, this area can be used for such things as TSRs and device drivers. This frees up more space in the lower 640K.

user-friendly Usually means bigger and more expensive. It should make using the computer easier. Memory is now less expensive, so large programs are being developed to use more memory than ever before.

user group Usually a club or a group of people who use computers. Often, the club is devoted to users of a certain type of computer. But in most clubs, anyone is welcome to join.

vaporware Products that are announced, usually with great fanfare, but are not yet ready for market.

virtual Something that might be essentially present, but not in actual fact. If you have a single disk drive, it is drive A:, but you also have a virtual drive B:. If you want to copy a file from one floppy to another on your single drive, you can use the command COPY A:filename B:filename (filename is the name of the file you want to copy).

virus Destructive code that is placed or embedded in a computer program. A virus is usually self-replicating and will often copy itself onto other programs. It might lie dormant for some time, then completely erase a person's hard disk.

volatile Refers to memory units such as RAM that lose stored information when power is removed. Nonvolatile memory is similar to that of ROM or a hard disk.

VRAM Video RAM. A type of special RAM used on video or monitor adapters. The better adapters have more memory so they can retain full-screen high-resolution images.

windows　Many new software packages are now loaded into memory. They stay in the background until they are called for, then they pop up on the screen in a window.

Windows 3.1　The excellent GUI program from Microsoft. It provides an operating environment for programs that makes them easier to use.

Index